Technology
and the Diverse
Learner

To Ellen

Who saw
Beauty in our Diversity
Unity in our Differences
Abilities in our Disabilities

Lessons taught to her friends, family, students, profession, and community.

Her inner light shines on in us all.

Technology and the Diverse Learner

A GUIDE to Classroom Practice

Marty Bray

Abbie Brown

Timothy D. Green

CORWIN PRESS, INC.
A Sage Publications Company
Thousand Oaks, California

For information:

Corwin Press
A Sage Publications Company
2455 Teller Road
Thousand Oaks, California 91320
www.corwinpress.com

Sage Publications Ltd.
1 Oliver's Yard
55 City Road
London EC1Y 1SP
United Kingdom

Sage Publications India Pvt. Ltd.
B-42, Panchsheel Enclave
Post Box 4109
New Delhi 110 017 India

Printed in the United States of America

Library of Congress Cataloging-in-Publication Data

Bray, Marty.
Technology and the diverse learner: A guide to classroom practice/Marty Bray, Abbie Brown, Timothy D. Green.
    p. cm.
Includes bibliographical references (p.) and index.
ISBN 0–7619–3171–6—ISBN 0–7619–3172–4 (pbk.)
  1. Special education—United States—Computer-assisted instruction.
2. Special education—United States—Data processing. 3. Inclusive education—United States. 4. Educational technology—United States. I. Brown, Abbie. II. Green, Timothy D., 1968- III. Title.
LC3969.5.B73 2004
371.9′04334—dc22

                        2003028175

04 05 06 07 10 9 8 7 6 5 4 3 2 1

Acquisitions Editor:	Robert D. Clouse
Editorial Assistant:	Candice L. Ling
Production Editor:	Melanie Birdsall
Copy Editor:	Interactive Composition Corporation
Typesetter:	C&M Digitals (P) Ltd.
Proofreader:	Cheryl Rivard
Indexer:	Michael Ferreira
Cover Designer:	Michael Dubowe
Graphic Designer:	Lisa Miller

Contents

Preface   vii

About the Authors   ix

1. **Looking at Gender, Culture, and Other Diversities
   in the Classroom: An Overview**   1
   Cultural Diversity   3
   Gender   5
   Differing Abilities: Exceptional Children   7
   Standards and Guidelines   15
   Summary   16
   For Further Application   17

2. **A Closer Look at Diverse Learners**   19
   English Language Learners/English
       as a Second Language Learners   20
   Learners With Physical Disabilities or Impairments   21
   Learners With Cognitive Impairments   24
   Students With Learning Disabilities   27
   Gifted and Talented Students   30
   Summary   30
   For Further Application   31

3. **Diverse Learners and Innovative Technologies**   33
   Assistive/Adaptive Technologies   34
   Supportive Technologies   46
   Remediation Technologies   47
   Compensatory Technologies   48
   Extension Technologies   50
   Summary   51
   For Further Application   52

4. **Curriculum, Technology, and Diverse Learners**   53
   Differentiated Instruction:
       What Is It and How Does It Work?   54

The Inclusive Classroom: An Overview   55
Technology and the Individual Education Plan   56
Cultural Sensitivity, Gender Equity, and the
    Use of Technology in the Classroom   59
Using Technology With ELL Students   60
Gender Equity and the Use of Technology   63
Using Technology in the Content Areas to
    Facilitate Instruction With Diverse Learners   64
Summary   76
For Further Application   76

Appendix A: Diverse Learners and Technologies   **79**

Appendix B: Diverse Learners and Instructional Strategies   **85**

References and Suggested Readings   **89**

Index   **95**

Preface

Classrooms are more diverse than ever. The inclusive classroom brings about a student population many teachers do not feel adequately prepared to handle. Innovative technologies can provide many types of support for diverse learners. We wrote this book to provide teachers with a practical guide that deals with the issues of how to make the best use of available technology to meet the needs of diverse learners. Our treatment of diverse learners includes issues related to culture, gender, and special needs (physical and/or mental disabilities). In this book we approach the subject from a practical point of view in a user-friendly manner.

This book is divided into four chapters. Chapter 1 is an overview of the issues associated with diverse learners in the classroom including standards and guidelines for using technology with a variety of diverse learners. Chapter 2 focuses on the characteristics of various categories of diverse learners. This chapter is designed to be an overview of the types of diverse learners that many of us have in our classrooms. Chapter 3 explores the different kinds of assistive/adaptive technologies available today. In addition to describing the technology itself, we discuss the kind of student who might benefit most from the technology. Chapter 4 discusses combinations of instructional strategies, technologies, and types of learners who would benefit most from the strategies described.

ACKNOWLEDGMENTS

The authors would like to thank the following people for their generous contributions of time and expertise that helped shape this book:

- Robb Clouse, acquisitions editor at Corwin Press, for supporting and shaping the ideas in this book
- Betty Youngkin, who put just the right touches on the dedication
- Ellen Bray, whose initial interest in her son's work turned into essential feedback and proofreading

Corwin Press gratefully acknowledges the contributions of the following individuals:

Barry Abbott
National Board Certified Teacher
Fannin County School System
Blue Ridge, Georgia

Sandra E. Archer
National Board Certified Teacher
Volusia County School District
Ormond Beach, Florida

Lauren Baah
Special Education Teacher
Irving High School
Irving, Texas

Nancy Blessing
National Board Certified Teacher
Sebastian Elementary School
Sebastian, Florida

Julie Box
National Board Certified Teacher
Colbert County School District
Muscle Shoals, Alabama

SiriNam S. Khalsa
National Board Certified Teacher
Springfield School District
Springfield, Massachusetts

Jorrie MacKensie
National Board Certified Teacher
Los Angeles Unified School District
Los Angeles, California

Lynn Semyck
National Board Certified Teacher
Madison City School District
Huntsville, Alabama

About the Authors

Marty Bray holds a Ph.D. in Instructional Systems Technology from Indiana University and an MLS from Appalachian State University. He also holds certification in the areas of behaviorally/emotionally disabled and academically gifted. In addition to working with exceptional children, Marty has worked as a media coordinator in North Carolina. Currently, he is an associate professor in the department of Elementary and Bilingual Education at California State University, Fullerton.

Abbie Brown holds a Ph.D. in Instructional Systems Technology from Indiana University and an MA from Teachers College at Columbia University. He is currently an associate professor at California State University, Fullerton, in the department of Elementary and Bilingual Education. He is coauthor of *Multimedia Projects in the Classroom: A Guide to Development and Evaluation* and a contributing author to *Teaching Strategies: A Guide to Effective Instruction.* He has taught at the Bank Street School for Children in New York City and George Washington Middle School in Ridgewood, New Jersey. He has received awards for outstanding teaching and curriculum design from the New Jersey Department of Education and is an experienced computer-based instructional media producer.

Timothy D. Green holds a Ph.D. in Instructional Systems Technology and Curriculum and Instruction from Indiana University. He is coauthor of *Multimedia Projects in the Classroom: A Guide to Development and Evaluation* and author of *PowerPoint Made Very Easy!* He has taught fourth grade and junior high school. His expertise is in multimedia design, the integration of technology into the teaching and learning process, and pedagogy. He is an assistant professor at California Sate University, Fullerton, in the department of Elementary and Bilingual Education. Currently, he is the university's director of Distance Education.

1 Looking at Gender, Culture, and Other Diversities in the Classroom

An Overview

Chapter Guiding Questions

This chapter will help you answer the following questions:

- How do cultural differences among students affect classroom experiences with new technologies?
- How is gender a factor among students using new technologies?
- How are disabilities differentiated and described?
- What are the standards and guidelines for working with technology in the classroom?
- What are the standards and guidelines for working with students with disabilities?

We are all different. Like snowflakes, no two human beings are exactly alike. How we recognize and relate to those differences depends on the prevailing culture, how individuals choose to make their needs known, and the technologies available to accommodate differences.

We educators must recognize that every student is unique. Differences among our students may be small or large. Some differences are considered advantageous (the "gifted" student) and give the student an advantage in the classroom. Other differences can be a challenge to the individual (the "disadvantaged" or "differently abled" student), especially in situations that highlight the challenge because of the emphasis on certain information-processing strategies.

A good example of how a challenge may also be a gift is the student with a learning disability who can master a concept but has difficulty reading the textbook because he or she is looking at the shapes on the page rather than decoding the meaning of the words on the page. In the classroom, where decoding text for meaning is critical, this is a serious problem. However, this "disability" becomes a "gift" when the student attends an art class or enrolls in a graphic design school where the ability to see the relationships among shapes is an asset.

This is a frustrating situation for all concerned. It is frustrating for students, who know that they understand the concept but cannot unlock the information. It is also frustrating for the teacher, who has to find different ways to help students unlock the information. Technology can be a big help to you, the teacher, in finding the right presentation strategy for the student. However, while technology can be a powerful tool, it has to be supported with effective instruction and, most important, by a knowledgeable and caring professional.

Innovations in information technologies and assistive/adaptive technologies can be powerful tools for success in the classroom. "Success" is defined as high achievement in the K–12 and higher-education curricula and/or in the workforce. As we continue to rely on computer technology at home and at work, equal access to this technology becomes critical to economic success (Gilley, 2002). This is another reason why the integration of technology in the classroom is important. By providing all students with access to technology in the regular classroom, you are also providing them with opportunities to gain skills that will serve them well after they leave school. While access to computers is getting better with time, many students are excluded from more advanced technology courses because of their gender, ethnicity, or disability. This digital divide (see Figure 1.1) limits the possibilities for these students, thus wasting their potential talent.

Although every individual is unique, some of the differences among us have been identified and categorized. The goal of making generalizations about differences is not to create stereotypes or support prejudices, but to identify the challenges and the gifts that many people share so that we may keep from overlooking, avoiding, or minimizing them. Our intent is to use these classifications as a way to help you find a technology or

---

Figure 1.1   The Digital Divide

In some instances the differences among individuals specifically concern their access to new technologies. The term "digital divide" refers to the gap between those in society who have access to computer technology and those who do not. Recognizing this problem and making new technologies a regular part of classroom activity reduce the digital divide and help all students succeed. Knowing what technology is capable of and how it can be used to foster student success is every teacher's responsibility.

---

method of instruction that can be a good fit. It is important to keep in mind that you may need to modify our suggestions and strategies to fit your unique situation. Throughout this book we will look at differences dictated by culture, gender, and ability because these are currently popular methods of categorizing the differences among individuals.

CULTURAL DIVERSITY

Whether we prefer to think of it as a "melting pot" or a "tossed salad," the population of the United States is composed of individuals from a variety of ethnic groups and cultures. Each of these groups and cultures contributes to creating a nation that is, we believe, greater than the sum of its parts. For all of the strengths derived from this variety, a heterogeneous society can present many challenges as well. Different languages, different customs, and the prejudices of one group against another can create impediments to educational success. Even agreeing on what it means to be a "successful" person can be difficult among varying groups.

Cultural differences are very real, but for the most part they have been constructed by society. That is to say, the differences we perceive are largely based on factors such as upbringing, training, and socioeconomic circumstance. Cultural differences can also be problematic because they are "in the eye of the beholder." Each individual identifies more with some aspects of his or her heritage than with other aspects. A person described by others as Eastern European American might identify himself or herself as American, Jewish, Catholic, New Yorker, or Californian. The possibilities for varying descriptions based on cultural differences are almost infinite and are made at the discretion of the individual. Few measures of cultural difference are truly objective, and intellectual or physical abilities are not inherent in individuals because of their cultural circumstances. One example of this phenomenon can be seen in cultures located in remote areas of the world that value survival skills such as building a fire and finding food. In this cultural (and physical) context, these skills are a mark of high intelligence. Fortunately for many educational researchers, survival skills are not as important in the United States, where mathematical intelligence is highly valued.

Two aspects of culture that can be measured to some extent are English language proficiency and socioeconomic status (SES). English language skill and SES have a particularly strong effect on how students are treated in the classroom and how they approach technology.

One's skill with the English language can have the greatest impact on the classroom experience for both student and teacher. There are well over two million non-English-speaking students in U.S. classrooms. During the 2000–01 school year, thirty-nine states reported supporting Limited English Proficiency (LEP) students (National Center for Education Statistics [NCES], 2003). California reported 1.5 million LEP students, and Texas reported more than half a million (NCES). LEP students are more motivated to learn English if they are attracted to the technology to begin with. This is in part due to the dominance of the English language on the Internet (see Figure 1.2).

Figure 1.2	Language Populations Online		
English	36.5%	Chinese	10.9%
Japanese	9.7%	Spanish	7.2%
German	6.7%	Korean	4.5%
Italian	3.8%	French	3.5%
Portuguese	3%	Russian	2.9%

SOURCE: European Travel Commission, *New Media Review.* Retrieved April 24, 2003, from http://www.etcnewmedia.com/review/.

Students' socioeconomic status (SES) can affect their experiences as learners as well. Obviously, low SES groups have less access to computing tools since these are currently expensive. Children from high SES families often have far more access to networked computers at home than do their low SES peers. It is interesting that students have access to the same video games and other forms of electronic entertainment regardless of their SES.

The way computing tools are used differently by high and low SES groups says a great deal about the availability of technology to high SES students and impacts their relationship with technology. High SES students are often placed in situations where they control the computer, using it for creative communication and data manipulation. On the other hand, low SES students are often subjected to computer programs that in essence control the individual; what is frequently referred to as "drill and practice" software limits the amount of personal power these students have over the computer so that they become passive, rather than active, participants in the instructional process (Butler-Pascoe & Wiburg, 2003).

Encouraging students from a variety of ethnic backgrounds can be challenging for the teacher. Many teachers who are successful in dealing with these issues provide not only access to technology but also role models (community members and/or celebrities) who demonstrate how people from similar backgrounds have successfully mastered technology in their lives and careers. These teachers show students how mastering technology can lead to higher-paying careers.

GENDER

Certainly one difference that can be measured among any human population is gender. Gender becomes a factor in classroom instruction when the teacher creates a learning environment that favors the success of either boys or girls. Most of the time the teacher's favoritism is subtle and unintentional. Historically, certain subject areas have tended to be problematic in terms of gender favoritism. Two curricular areas where gender is problematic are science and technology.

Gender differences are both similar to and different from cultural differences. Certainly there are physiological differences between the sexes, but these do not extend to inherent differences in the ability to succeed at school or work. The effect of gender on learning and achievement is constructed by culture. In Western societies, girls are expected to behave more passively than boys. Boys are expected to be active and curious, often to the point of getting into trouble, which is considered normal and acceptable (Schrum & Geisler, 2003). Typically, our culture describes "male" behavior as aggressive, assertive, and competitive. "Female" behavior is described as collaborative and supportive. Boys are encouraged to develop skills in fields like engineering and computer science; girls are often discouraged from participation in these fields. Fields that focus on personal aesthetics (e.g., fashion and interior design) and child development (e.g., elementary education) are considered a female realm.

From these differences come disparate approaches to technology. Research conducted by Honey et al. (1991) suggests that males envision technology as a means to gain power and control over the physical universe, while females envision technology as a means to improve communication and collaboration.

Currently, males use computing technologies more often than girls. Boys use computers as toys, while girls use computers to accomplish tasks

(Gilley, 2002). Research shows that girls are just as capable as boys at handling computer technology. However, research also shows that boys tend to receive greater encouragement from parents and teachers to pursue computer interests than girls (Margolis & Fisher, 2001). Boys tend to become "obsessed" with computers whereas girls tend to be occasional users. This difference in approach seems to create situations in which boys are encouraged to develop expertise with computing technologies (Margolis & Fisher, 2001). Moreover, women tend to have a lower self-perception of their real computer skills than do men (Mathis, 2002).

Historically, not many women have entered the field of information technology (IT) (Mathis, 2002). Yet many jobs require technical expertise but not the traditional programming skills that most people associate with IT careers. Graphic arts is a career path that does not involve programming and yet is technology intensive. Graphic artists use computers to create original artwork for print, video, and the Web. Computers play a key role in television and filmmaking. Today, many movies we see feature backgrounds, action, and even characters that are created in the computer. The same is true for many animated movies, such as *Toy Story*. Theatrical production can also involve a great deal of computer technology. The control of lighting and sound is often managed with some type of computer interface. Teaching is yet another area in which technology can be an important tool. Increasingly, community colleges and universities have departments of distance education that help instructors develop and deliver their teaching online. Professionals in this area have a unique blend of people and technology skills. Although they have not been popularly adopted, several initiatives are currently under way to explore the possibilities of teaching online in K–12 settings.

With all of these career possibilities open to girls and boys, it is important that teachers become aware of gender issues and work to make opportunities available for both boys and girls to learn more about technology. A key to this, of course, is an awareness of the "gender factor" in your classroom. There are several possible approaches, but one simple way of doing this is to occasionally videotape your classroom, focusing the camera on the technology. After videotaping the activities in your classroom over a period of days, review the videotapes to see how often students are using the technology, who is using it, and how they are using it. Once you have done this, you can identify problems and correct them. You may notice that when working in groups, the boys tend to "hog" the keyboard and the girls are frequently forced to sit off to the side and engage in other activities. If this occurs, you can establish group rules that require the girls to be on the keyboard for the same amount of time as the boys. You can also rotate roles in the group to ensure that the girls have a certain number of tasks to do on the computer.

DIFFERING ABILITIES: EXCEPTIONAL CHILDREN

Cultural and gender differences are things we all share. Each of us claims a heritage and each of us can be defined as either male or female. At some point many of us can also claim the further distinction of being "exceptional." For most of us, this will happen later in life when we face a medical condition such as arthritis that can leave us impaired or disabled. For a significant number of us, being exceptional is a characteristic that spans an entire lifetime. Individuals who are considered exceptional are defined as having impairments and/or talents that place them at an unusual point on the spectrum of human ability.

While every individual is slightly different in his or her cognitive and physical abilities, exceptional children have skills and abilities that are unusually different. Some may have significant cognitive impairments that limit their ability to encode or decode information, while others may have superior ability in retaining information or in generalizing existing knowledge to new situations. Some students may have significant physical impairments that limit their hearing, vision, or motor skills. Often we think of exceptional children as those with cognitive and physical challenges, but gifted and talented individuals are considered exceptional as well.

Since it is common to address first the needs of students who face challenges, we will begin by defining key terms that are frequently used to differentiate conditions (see Figure 1.3). It is important to reemphasize that although someone may have an impairment, he or she does not necessarily have a disability.

Figure 1.3   Defining the Differences Among Exceptional Individuals

The Americans with Disabilities Act (ADA) provides descriptions that essentially define the following:

Impairment. A problem with or loss of normal psychological or anatomical functioning.

Disability. A restriction in or loss of one's ability to perform normal human activities.

Handicapped (Disadvantaged). A situation in which a person's age, sex, social, or cultural status prevents that person from fulfilling a role considered normal for him or her.

A fourth difference not defined by the ADA is:

Gifted and Talented. Displaying highly superior abilities in memory, cognitive reasoning, visual skills, or auditory skills.

There are four terms commonly used to identify exceptional individuals: *impairment, disability, disadvantaged,* and *gifted and talented.*

An impairment is a problem with or the loss of normal mental or physical functions. A student who is impaired may be missing a limb or lack the ability to hear. A student who has a cognitive impairment may have difficulties memorizing a list of spelling words.

A disabled student is limited in or cannot perform normal human activities, such as walking or reading. While there is significant debate over the characteristics of specific disabilities, there are four commonly accepted broad groups of disabilities:

- Learning, which includes dyslexia (reading), dysgraphia (writing), and dyscalculia (mathematics)
- Speech and language
- Mental retardation
- Emotional disturbance

Students are considered to be disadvantaged when their disability creates problems for them in specific situations. An example is the learning disabled child in the classroom. The normal classroom environment requires a great deal of reading and writing for a student to be successful. A student with dyslexia is disadvantaged in this environment because to be successful the student needs to do a great deal of reading. However, in a situation such as graphic design, the same student would not be disadvantaged because reading does not have the same impact on the student's success.

Exceptional children are varied, and in an attempt to deal with their educational needs, educators have developed several "categories" to describe the impairments of these children. Although many exceptional children have some type of impairment, they can also fall into the category of gifted and talented. While some misuse these categories by assigning labels to children and discriminating against them, the labels are intended to help in describing the types of services that tend to be most beneficial to students who fall within these broad categories.

The definitions of many categories such as "learning disability" are still being debated within the exceptional education community. This speaks volumes about the diversity of learners who fall under the umbrella term "exceptional children." For the purposes of this book, we will use three broad areas to help us organize the various types of exceptionalities: *physical impairments, cognitive impairments,* and *gifted and talented.*

- Physical impairments affect mobility and/or limit a student's interaction with the learning environment based on information processing.

Examples of physical impairments that affect mobility include spina bifida, muscular dystrophy, and spinal cord injuries. Examples of physical impairments that influence a student's ability to interact with the learning environment and process information include vision or hearing loss (to the point that the student has trouble reading or hearing the teacher).

- Cognitive impairments can impede a student's ability to process information. Types of cognitive impairments include traumatic brain injury, autism, mental retardation, behavioral disorders, communication disorders, and learning disorders. Students who have cognitive impairments may have difficulty processing language or memorizing. Aphasia is a communication disorder that limits a student's ability to process language (usually associated with a stroke). A student who has aphasia may be able to recognize objects in pictures but will not be able to name those objects. An example of a learning disorder is attention deficit hyperactivity disorder (ADHD), which limits a student's ability to attend to and stay focused on a specific activity. A student who has ADHD tends to be restless and to move from one activity to another without completing the first activity.

- Gifted and talented refers to students who excel in academic settings and therefore require unique instructional strategies to address their "accelerated" needs. A student who is identified as gifted and talented displays remarkable abilities that go far beyond the standard range of abilities found among most people. A person may be gifted and talented in terms of cognitive skill (memory, reasoning, or rote functions such as multiplication or division), visual or auditory skills (the visual or musical arts), or physical skill (athletic ability or an enhanced sense).

Technology can be quite effective in reducing or removing restrictions that hinder the performance of normal human activities. Word processing, for example, can simplify many writing tasks such as spell checking. In the early 1980s, many studies were conducted that examined new ways of composing on the computer. At the time, functions such as spell checking were considered novel and came as separate programs to be used with the word processor. For many students with learning disabilities, word processing was a blessing that allowed them the freedom to get their thoughts down without having to use pencil and paper. Now, word processing is found in most office environments. Spell check is now integrated into virtually all word processors and even into Web browsers such as Apple's *Safari,* which allows an individual to spell-check the contents of a form before it is submitted. Many other technologies are following the same path, including computerized speech that can be used to read the contents of Web sites back to a student.

Word processing is a great example of a technology that can support a student with a disability. Three distinct types of technological or strategic support that can help reduce or remove restrictions for students with disabilities are *assistive/adaptive, remedial,* and *compensatory.* One interesting thing about these categories is that the same technology can fall into a different category depending on the context in which it is being used.

- Assistive/adaptive technologies and strategies assist students with a task that they cannot accomplish otherwise. Assistive technologies can be simple or complicated. A straw that helps a paralyzed person drink from a glass is an example of a simple assistive technology. A computerized wheelchair that can be controlled by blowing into a mouthpiece is an example of a complicated assistive technology. Assistive/adaptive technologies are generally not used to teach a concept but are used to help the student access the information necessary to learn the concept (e.g., eyeglasses do not help a child learn to read; they help a child see well enough to learn to read).

- Remedial technologies and strategies teach or remediate. Like traditional remediation, remediation technologies use repetition and simplification of complex concepts to "remediate" the student. Examples include software designed to help students practice specific skills such as spelling, reading, or mathematics. Remedial technologies are easy to use in the classroom, as they require little input from the teacher. But they do require that the teacher understand the instructional needs of students and the capabilities of the software to make an effective match between the two. Teachers may be tempted to overuse a remedial technology because it appears to do all of the work for them. To avoid falling into this trap, teachers must carefully assess when the need for the software has passed and when activities that encourage the development of higher-order thinking are necessary.

- Compensatory technologies and strategies help a student perform an academic task more effectively and efficiently than they could on their own. Examples include word processing (instead of handwriting), spell-checking software, and calculators. These tools are assistive in that they help the student accomplish a task; they are also teaching tools in that they help the student better understand certain concepts. Using a graphic calculator to teach statistical concepts is a good example. The student can perform simple operations while learning how more complex operations work.

How Many Exceptional Children Are There?

Approximately 8.8% of the population ages six to seventeen is receiving special education services. This percentage translates into approximately 5.7 million students. Most of the students receiving special education services are between three and nine years old. The number of students receiving these services gradually decreases after students reach age nine (Heward, 2003). There are many reasons why students no longer need services. Some students appear to "grow out" of an exceptional category or develop "coping" strategies that allow them to function effectively in an educational environment. Other students are "cured" because of effective interventions early in their educational career. Regardless of the reasons, exceptional students still need effective classroom instruction that meets their needs.

Students with learning disabilities make up 50% of the children identified as exceptional. This is the fastest-growing group; 18.9% of the exceptional population has a speech/language impairment; 10.6% has some form of mental retardation; and 8.2% has some type of emotional disturbance U.S. Department of Education, 2002). While students with emotional disabilities make up the smallest number of exceptional students, they tend to require many more resources.

Although law does not mandate it, forty-three states currently provide services for gifted and talented students. More than two million students are receiving these services.

History of the Legislation Regarding Disabilities

Prior to the 1970s, many states had laws that excluded students with disabilities from mainstream classrooms. These students were often relegated to school basements or separate buildings. The recognition that unequal educational opportunities existed for these students led to legislation known as PL 94–142/IDEA.

Originally called the Education for All Handicapped Children Act, PL 94–142/IDEA was passed in 1975 and has been amended several times since its enactment. A 1990 amendment renamed the original legislation the Individuals with Disabilities Education Act, or IDEA. In 1997, provisions concerning issues such as increased parental participation were included in the legislation (U.S. Department of Education, 2003). There had been other legislation prior to it, but IDEA's six principles are considered the most comprehensive and sweeping of any legislation protecting students with disabilities:

- Schools must educate *all* children with disabilities.
- Schools must use nonbiased, scientific methods to identify students with disabilities.
- Students are entitled to free and appropriate public education.

- Students must be educated in the least restrictive environment possible (this means that students must remain in the regular classroom as much as possible).
- Schools must have due process safeguards such as parental consent before placement can occur.
- Parents and students must be involved in a shared decision-making process before placement can occur. This is often done through annual Individual Education Plan (IEP) meetings. IDEA is the first legislation that required an IEP for each child.

While each of these principles is important, the concept of the least restrictive environment (LRE) probably has the greatest impact on the classroom teacher. Traditionally, LRE has meant that students went to a special classroom for additional services. The popularity of the recent movement *inclusion* means that more students stay in the mainstream classroom and resources are brought to them. Inclusion requires effective planning between the classroom teacher and the resource teacher and flexibility from the classroom teacher. However, when carried out correctly, inclusion allows students to benefit from a full day of instruction and integration with their peers.

Another legislative act, the Gifted and Talented Children's Education Act of 1978, provides funds for inservice training programs and research aimed at meeting the needs of gifted and talented students. Like IDEA, this act has been amended several times. As with LRE, the challenge for the classroom teacher is to provide instruction that meets the needs of the student identified as gifted in the context of the classroom. Within the classroom environment, the teacher has to augment the regular instruction for the gifted and talented student.

The Americans with Disabilities Act (ADA), enacted in 1990, is landmark legislation that extends the civil rights protection of persons with disabilities to all public services including transportation and telecommunications and to private sector employment. This is significant because in addition to affecting classroom instruction, the act protects all people with disabilities at every stage of life from discrimination. Among other things, the ADA affects the accessibility of Web sites, through Titles II and III, which require state and local governments and others to provide effective communication whenever the Internet is used (International Center for Disability Resources on the Internet, 1999). The accessibility of Web sites is important for classroom teachers when they are selecting online resources to use in their classroom. Visually impaired students can use readers that can read the contents of a Web site to them. However, if the Web site does not conform to accessibility standards (and many do not), they will be of little instructional use.

The Individual Education Plan (IEP)

The IEP is a critical part of the special education process. The IEP is a system for determining where the child is and where he or she should be going. The IEP is important for the classroom teacher because it specifies how the student will achieve educational goals, how long the attainment of those goals should take, and how everyone will know when the child achieves those goals. IDEA requires that every student with special needs between the ages of three and twenty-one have an IEP. Older students must have a provision in their IEP to help them make the transition out of school. This transition could be toward independent living, including, if possible, some type of work after school is completed.

An IEP is created by a designated IEP team that must include the student's parent(s), at least one regular education teacher, at least one special education teacher, a representative from the local education agency (LEA), an individual who can interpret the instructional implications of evaluation results (generally a school psychologist), other individuals such as outside tutors who are familiar with the education of the child (this is at the discretion of the parents or school), and the student if he or she is age fourteen or older.

The regular education teacher plays an important role in the development and implementation of the IEP. In many cases, it is the classroom teacher who makes the initial referral when it becomes apparent that a student is having difficulty in school. The regular classroom teacher can also provide the IEP team with a great deal of feedback about the student's progress.

Individual Education Plans have a variety of components. Many are required by law and are designed to ensure that the rights of students are not violated and that they receive the best and most appropriate services possible. The parts of the IEP that are directly concerned with instruction include the following:

- The student's current educational performance
- Goals and objectives that are measurable along with benchmarks that can indicate progress
- Services that the student will receive, including special and regular education and any supplemental services
- Program modifications that may have to be made to support the student
- The extent, if any, to which the student will not participate in the regular class

The IEP also specifies any modifications that may be required for standardized tests such as state-administered achievement tests. These modifications can include extra time, word processing, and/or a person to read the test to the student. The type of testing modifications allowed can vary depending on the state where the student resides. All Individual Education Plans, however, must include a rationale for any modifications to the administration of standardized tests and alternate methods of assessment if a standardized assessment is not appropriate. These modifications can have significant ramifications for the student if, for instance, certain modifications mean that the student does not graduate from high school but receives a certificate of completion instead. Needless to say, these important decisions should involve the entire IEP team.

The IEP also includes several items that measure the student's progress and establish procedures:

- The projected date for the beginning of the services and modifications described
- The anticipated frequency, location, and duration of services and modifications
- How the team will measure the student's progress toward yearly goals
- How parents will be regularly informed about their child's progress
- Whether the progress that the student makes is sufficient to meet annual goals

The IEP can include statements about the student's use of assistive technologies for instruction including computing tools such as word-processing and spell-checking software, specialized input devices (keyboards, tablets, mice, touch screens), text readers for books and/or for online resources (e.g., Web sites), and software tutorial programs for spelling, reading, and math.

Inclusion

The term "inclusion" means educating students with disabilities in regular classrooms. This is part of the least restrictive environment principle of IDEA: students must be educated as close to the regular educational environment as possible. In practice, inclusion means that instead of pulling the exceptional child out of the classroom, services are brought to the child in the classroom. Some experts believe in full inclusion in which all children with disabilities are served in the regular classroom, while others (including the Council for Exceptional Children) believe in a continuum of inclusion with full inclusion as the ultimate goal. The child's IEP should determine the degree to which inclusion is accomplished.

Inclusion in educational settings has several defining characteristics (Giangreco, Cloninger, Dennis, & Edelman, 2000). Among these are:

- The inclusion of students with a variety of abilities
- Students feeling that they are an integral part of the classroom
- Students sharing a common education experience
- Persons with and without disabilities equally sharing the setting
- Addressing the needs of the entire student (social, psychological, etc.)

While the degree to which inclusion should take place is still being debated, it is proving to be a successful educational strategy for many students with disabilities. Of course, a key component to the success or failure of inclusion is whether the classroom teacher is able and/or willing to differentiate instruction to meet the individual needs of students in the classroom.

STANDARDS AND GUIDELINES

Standards provide educators with guidelines intended to promote best practices in a particular subject or field. The standards we will concern ourselves with most closely throughout this book directly relate to technology in the classroom, to special education, and to issues of accessibility as it relates to information technology.

The International Society for Technology in Education (ISTE) has set forth the most popular and widely accepted classroom technology standards. Thirty states have adopted the society's *National Educational Technology Standards for Students* (the NETS-S). The ISTE standards specify what students should know in order to be technologically literate. The most important standards center around the use of technology to support issues related to diversity and to personal productivity in the classroom:

- Students understand the ethical, cultural, and societal issues related to technology.
- Students use technology tools to enhance learning, increase productivity, and promote creativity (International Society for Technology in Education, 2000).

IDEA does not provide any standards as such but does contain many guidelines for the use of technology with exceptional children including assistive technology, technology to create a least restrictive environment, and instruction and assessment. IDEA also provides guidelines for IEP development, which is important in determining appropriate use of technology in the classroom.

The ADA mandates that persons with disabilities be given equal access to all public places and institutions. All federally funded projects have to provide this accessibility. Web accessibility is one of the most widely impacted subjects of this mandate. This is also relevant to the instruction that takes place in the classroom if it involves technology. Asking a student with a visual impairment to use a Web site that does not meet basic accessibility standards can create many problems for the student. Fortunately, most Web sites that are accessible proudly display one or more "seals of approval" such as the "Bobby Approved" icon (*Bobby* is software that analyzes Web sites and Web pages to determine whether all accessibility standards have been met; for more information on *Bobby*, visit http://bobby.cast.org/). Since many schools have Web sites of their own, it is critically important to follow guidelines for Web accessibility in order to be ADA compliant. This is especially true if the school receives federal funding. Specific guidelines and tools are available from the World Wide Web Consortium (W3C) at http://www.w3c.org/.

SUMMARY

We need only to walk into a clothing store to see that human beings come in all shapes and sizes. We need only to spend time in a classroom to see that students also come in all ("instructional") shapes and sizes. In this chapter, we have explored cultural, gender, physical, and cognitive differences that students possess. Many of the problems related to culture and gender tend to emerge when teachers are unaware of how the classroom environment and/or their own behaviors support or hinder students as they interact with technology.

Students can have a variety of exceptionalities that can arise from some type of impairment or an unusual talent. Technology can provide the teacher with tools that can facilitate assistance, remediation, or extended learning.

In the United States, exceptional students are protected by several laws, including IDEA and the ADA. IDEA mandates that every student with an exceptionality must have an Individual Education Plan. This plan sets instructional goals and defines the modifications and support necessary to reach these goals. The concept of least restrictive environment first mandated by IDEA is today being expanded through the practice of inclusion.

Standards and guidelines provided by the ADA, IDEA, and the International Society for Technology in Education, while not overly specific, inform the best practices of using technology to accommodate diverse learners.

FOR FURTHER APPLICATION

Below are several resources and professional development activities that can help you better understand how technology can be used with diverse learners.

- Teaching Diverse Learners (http://www.lab.brown.edu/tdl/) is one of many Web sites that can provide information and links to additional resources to help you better understand the pedagogical issues associated with English Language Learners. Of special interest are the many events listed on the Web site.

- The Council for Exceptional Children (http://www.cec.sped.org/) is the leading organization for exceptional children. In addition to its Web site, which offers a great deal of information and many links to resources about exceptional children, the council holds a number of workshops and an annual conference.

- Many organizations provide Web sites, list serves, and discussion forums that can help you communicate with experts and other teachers who have worked with diverse learners. Using a search engine such as Google (www.google.com), you can search for diverse learner listservers to find many discussion forums.

- One way to learn more about diverse learners is to take a course on the subject, and courses offered online may be particularly well suited to professionals with time and geographic constraints. A Google search using the terms "online course," "diverse," and "learners" will take you to several sites that list or offer online courses that focus on instruction for diverse learners. One such Web site is the Learning Bridges Online Learning Center (http://www.learningbridges.com/PDSChar.aspx), which offers both free and fee-based online courses. Many of these courses can be taken during the summer and may count as professional development.

2 A Closer Look at Diverse Learners

Chapter Guiding Questions

This chapter will help you answer the following questions:

- What are the characteristics typical of English Language Learners?
- What are the characteristics typical of learners identified as learning disabled?
- What are the characteristics typical of learners with physical impairments?
- What are the characteristics typical of learners with cognitive impairments?
- What are the characteristics typical of learners identified as gifted and talented?

Meeting the needs of diverse learners is a challenging opportunity. It takes a sophisticated level of knowledge, skill, and training that many teachers often feel they lack, which makes them feel unprepared to work effectively with diverse learners. You may be a member of this group. Fortunately, many resources (technological and human) exist that can help you take on this challenge. As with all challenges, knowledge is the place to start. To be successful with diverse learners, you need to be able to identify their characteristics and attributes. The more you understand these learners, the greater the chance that their needs will be met and that a supportive atmosphere fostering improvement, achievement, and satisfaction for everyone will be created. Such an environment is not only rewarding for the student, but can be immensely rewarding for you as well.

For the purposes of this book, we will focus on five categories of diverse learners that you may have in your classroom at some time:

- English Language Learners/English as a Second Language Learners
- Learners with physical disabilities
- Learners with cognitive disabilities
- Learners with learning disabilities
- Learners identified as gifted and talented

When you approach the needs of a unique learner, it is always important to seek out the strengths of the learner as well as to strive to meet the challenges. Oftentimes these challenges are created when there is a mismatch between what can be a rather rigid educational environment and the student's set of unique needs. Frequently you can meet these challenges with simple modifications to your classroom that can allow the student to fully realize his or her potential once you understand the characteristics unique to the student.

ENGLISH LANGUAGE LEARNERS/ENGLISH AS A SECOND LANGUAGE LEARNERS

In most of the United States, students whose primary language is not English are attending school in ever greater numbers (Shore, 1998). These students are often referred to as English Language Learners (ELL), sometimes called English as a Second Language (ESL). For the remainder of this book, we will refer to them as ELL students. These students constitute a significant percentage of the U.S. student population. As of 1990, nearly 6.3 million students between the ages of five and seventeen did not speak English as their primary language (ERIC Digests, 1993). Schools currently provide programs for nearly two million ELL students (Butler-Pascoe & Wiburg, 2003).

More than likely, the ELL students you encounter will have difficulties adjusting to a school environment. There are many reasons for this, but because English Language Learners do not have the same mastery of English as non-ELL students, they are at a disadvantage in the classroom. Therefore, they are classified as diverse learners. It is important to know that while some ELL students may have other disabilities, most do not.

While fluency in English is the primary problem, many ELL students do not master English at the same rate as other students because of factors such as field independence, socioeconomic status (SES), and internal locus of control (Diaz, 2001). This leads to many problems for ELL students including poor skills in reading, writing, and math. It may also impair the student's ability to develop and maintain social relationships.

Unfortunately, many states have recently instituted limits on the amount of time that ELL students can receive instruction in speaking and reading English and have mandated that ELL students be quickly mainstreamed into the regular classroom (Thompson, Dicerbo, Mahoney, & MacSwan, 2002).

This presents a challenge for you, but there are several strategies that you can use to meet it. These strategies include having other students in the class experience a lesson in a foreign language, providing opportunities for success, encouraging ELL students to improve their native language fluency, encouraging family involvement in the student's education, and learning about other cultures in your classroom (Shore, 1998).

Technology can be an effective tool to help ELL students work on their verbal interactions, vocabulary development, and reading skills (Ybarra & Green, 2003). Computer-aided instruction can provide ELL students with focused opportunities to develop English language skills while freeing the teacher to continue working with other students in the classroom. Other technologies such as e-mail and the World Wide Web can link ELL students with students from their native culture.

LEARNERS WITH PHYSICAL DISABILITIES OR IMPAIRMENTS

Students, like everyone else, can have a wide variety of physical impairments. Some of these impairments can be so severe that they are classified as disabilities. During the 2000–01 school year, 8.8% of the school-age population (ages six to seventeen) received exceptional children's services (Heward, 2003). While this percentage is relatively low, the number of students with physical disabilities is significant. Impairments and the physical conditions that cause them include the following:

Cerebral Palsy

Cerebral palsy (CP) is a disorder that affects an individual's control of his or her muscles. It is the most prevalent physical disability in school-age children. Children with cerebral palsy have experienced a brain injury that prevents them from using some of the muscles in their body in what is considered to be a normal manner. A child with CP may have little or no control over their arms, legs, or speech. This makes simple tasks such as walking, talking, and eating extremely difficult (Hallahan & Kauffman, 2000).

Despite what many think, cerebral palsy is not a disease or illness. It is not contagious, nor does it get worse. CP is not a condition the student will "outgrow"; it is a condition the student will have for his or her lifetime.

It is also important to recognize that muscle control and intelligence are not necessarily related (Heward, 2003).

Children with CP can have normal intelligence. Of course, they may also exhibit mild or even severe cognitive impairments. While it can be difficult to separate these two functions, it is important to do so when working with students who have CP if they are to receive the best education possible.

Spina Bifida

Spina bifida is a condition in which there is an incomplete closure in the spinal column. This condition prevents the nerves that are used to control and sense (feel) the lower body from properly forming. The severity of spina bifida depends on the amount of damage to the spinal cord. When the damage to the spinal cord is mild, the student experiences few problems and it may not even be apparent that the student has spina bifida. Unfortunately, for many students with spina bifida, the damage is more severe. These students may have severe impairments including poor coordination and/or the inability to walk (Heward, 2003; Lutkenhoff, 1999; Lutkenhoff & Oppenheimer, 1997; McLone, 1998; National Information Center for Children and Youth with Disabilities, 2003; Sandler, 1997).

For these students, learning problems do not revolve around cognitive functioning but around physical access. To address these problems, the teacher can arrange the classroom so as to be wheelchair accessible and/or provide modified keyboards and mice.

Muscular Dystrophy

Muscular dystrophy (MD) is a group of inherited diseases marked by progressive wasting away or atrophy of an individual's muscles. A child with MD may have difficulty moving his or her feet after lying down or playing on the floor. Additionally, a student with MD may easily fall. Tragically, MD is a fatal condition that tends to manifest itself early in the child's life (two to four years). By the ages of ten to fourteen, the child typically loses the ability to walk. Usually the last muscles to be affected are those in the hand (Sirvis, 1988, as cited in Friend & Bursuck, 1996), which means that the student can continue to engage in activities such as writing after mobility has been affected. As is true of CP, many technologies such as motorized wheelchairs are available to help with mobility.

Spinal Cord Injuries

Spinal cord injuries, like CP, usually result from direct damage to the spinal cord. As with CP, the area where the injury occurs affects the type and degree of impairment.

Vehicular accidents, sports injuries, and violence are the most common causes of spinal cord injuries of school-age children. Given the types of accidents that most frequently cause spinal cord injuries, it is not surprising that boys and young males between the ages of fifteen and thirty are most likely (80%) to have a spinal cord injury (National Spinal Cord Injury Association, 2001).

Visual Impairments

Students with visual disabilities are a very small part of the school-age population. Approximately 25,927 students between the ages of six and twenty-one received services under IDEA in 2000–01 (U.S. Department of Education, 2002). There are many causes of visual impairment. They can be present from birth or can be the result of disease or accident. Unfortunately, students with visual impairments can also have problems with language because they do not have visual cues that can help them interpret subtle messages inherent in spoken language. While this does not necessarily restrict the child, it does emphasize the need for repeated direct contact with concepts and information through nonvisual senses (Heward, 2003).

Students with a range of visual disabilities can also have problems with motor development and mobility because activities such as walking are in part dependent on visual cues. In addition to problems with motor development and mobility, students with visual disabilities can experience a degree of social detachment because of their physical limitation. It is important to know that visual disabilities have both legal and educational definitions. An individual who is *legally blind* can see from 20 feet what a normal-sighted person can see from 200 feet. This is important as some students are able to function quite well in an academic environment at 20/200 or even 20/400 with some minor assistance.

Educationally blind students are visually impaired to the point that they cannot function in a normal educational setting. Three types of blindness are related to the term "educationally blind": total blindness, functionally blind, and low vision. Totally blind students are unable to see any useful information. Students who are functionally blind have so little vision that they must learn primarily through auditory and tactile methods with only supplemental visual information.

Hearing Impairments

During the 2000–01 school year, 70,622 students with hearing impairments were served under IDEA (U.S. Department of Education, 2002). One of the characteristics of hearing impairments is that the degree of hearing loss occurs on a continuum and so can vary greatly from student to student. Students with mild hearing impairments are able to understand normal speech. On the other end of the scale is complete deafness. Because of this wide range, students who are designated as having hearing loss are an extremely heterogeneous group and therefore share very few common characteristics in how they learn best. Students with hearing impairments are at a disadvantage when learning English and its subtleties. They have difficulties learning speech because they are unable to monitor volume or control and they have poor inflection.

Students with hearing impairments also often experience feelings of isolation. It is important to know that these feelings tend to be worse for students with mild hearing loss rather than for those with profound hearing loss as many teachers may assume the opposite (ASHA, 2001, as cited in Heward, 2003).

LEARNERS WITH COGNITIVE IMPAIRMENTS

Students can exhibit a wide range of cognitive impairments from slight to very severe. When you are working with students with cognitive impairments, it is important to be careful not to assume the degree to which a student is limited by a specific condition. As with the human condition, impairments are also like snowflakes, because they are highly variable. This variability is one of the reasons why experts use categories and why we will focus on those impairments for which assistive technologies are readily available.

Traumatic Brain Injury

The number of children with traumatic brain injury (TBI) being served in schools is relatively small: 14,829 (U.S. Department of Education, 2002). TBI is a type of brain injury that results from an external physical force such as a concussion caused by child abuse or an auto accident (Hallahan & Kauffman, 2000).

Children with TBI may lack coordination, short-term memory, long-term memory, organizational skills, and impaired speech. Students with TBI may also have behavioral problems such as mood swings, self-centeredness, and lack of motivation (Heward, 2003).

Autism

Autism is widely considered to be a developmental disability that affects verbal and nonverbal communication as well as social interaction. Children with autism typically engage in repetitive activities and movements such as rocking. They also become highly agitated with any change in environment, daily routines, or unusual stimuli (Friend & Bursuck, 1996). For example, autistic students may become extremely upset when approached by a stranger or when they have to change classrooms.

As with other cognitive disabilities, relatively few students are diagnosed with autism. During the 2000–01 school year, 78,717 students were served under IDEA for autism (U.S. Department of Education, 2002). It is also important to know that boys are four times more likely than girls to be diagnosed with autism (Fombonne, 1999).

Mental Retardation

The U.S. Department of Education (2002) estimates that 1% (611,878) of the school-age population can be classified as having mental retardation. However, mental retardation is a condition that defies a clear-cut definition.

IDEA uses a definition of mental retardation that identifies students as mentally retarded if they demonstrate a subaverage general intellectual functioning along with deficits in adaptive behavior. These impairments manifest themselves during the development period and adversely affect the child's educational performance (Heward, 2003).

The American Association on Mental Retardation (AAMR) defines mental retardation as a "disability characterized by significant limitations in both intellectual functioning and conceptual, social, and practical adaptive skills" (AAMR, 1992, as cited in Heward, 2003). This definition is important because it recognizes the significance of cultural and environmental contexts when making a diagnosis. The AAMR also recognizes that limitations and strengths coexist in every individual, and that with appropriate individualized supports, functioning will improve.

The AAMR (1992, p. 203) has identified four levels of support that can guide the type and intensity of instructional and technical interventions:

- *Intermittent.* Support is provided when needed.
- *Limited.* Support is low intensity (not daily) but consistent over a sustained period.
- *Extensive.* Daily support is provided over a long period.
- *Pervasive.* Daily support that involves potentially life-sustaining activities is provided.

Students classified as mentally retarded may have problems with a variety of academic skills including memory, attention, generalization of learning, and motivation. Additionally, students with mental retardation often have significant problems with adaptive behavior, such as self-care/daily living skills, social development, and other appropriate behavior (e.g., accepting criticism, limited self-control) (Heward, 2003).

Interventions/assistive technologies such as computer programs that provide consistent positive feedback and management systems that help the teacher manage student behavior are appropriate for students with mental retardation (Heward, 2003).

Behavioral Disorders

All children may engage in inappropriate behaviors from time to time. Children with behavioral disorders exhibit inappropriate behaviors with intensity and frequency that are far outside what is considered to be normal. IDEA estimates that 0.7% (472,932) of school-age children with behavioral disorders were served during the 2000–01 school year (U.S. Department of Education, 2002).

Like mental retardation, a widely accepted definition of what constitutes a behavioral disorder does not exist. This can be attributed to varying definitions as to what constitutes "normal" or "acceptable" classroom behavior. Researchers do agree that there are many causes for behavioral disorders including biological causes, pathological family relationships, poor school experiences, and negative cultural influences (Hallahan & Kauffman, 2000). This is important as the interventions that can help can vary depending on the cause of the impairment.

Despite a widely accepted definition, it is agreed that children with behavioral disorders exhibit a number of antisocial behaviors such as:

- Getting out of their seats (at inappropriate times and frequently)
- Yelling, talking out, or cursing
- Disturbing their peers
- Hitting or fighting
- Ignoring the teacher
- Complaining
- Arguing excessively
- Stealing
- Lying
- Destroying property
- Not complying with directions
- Having temper tantrums
- Being excluded from peer-controlled activities
- Not responding to teacher corrections
- Not completing assignments
- Acting aggressive or withdrawn (Walker, 1997, as cited in Heward, 2003)

Because of these behaviors, most students with behavioral disorders often perform below grade level academically (Hallahan & Kauffman, 2000).

Communication Disorders

Communication disorders can be thought of as an inability to properly send, receive, and/or process verbal and nonverbal information. Communication disorders can affect speech, verbal comprehension, and written comprehension. Speech impairments are an example of a communication disorder. Fortunately, there are several instructional and technological innovations, such as remedial, multimedia-based software, available for these students.

During the 2000–01 school year, 2.3% (1,092,105) of school-age children received services for communication disorders (U.S. Department of Education, 2002). Communication is such a central part of human existence that communication disorders present a serious impediment in students' ability to function in the classroom.

STUDENTS WITH LEARNING DISABILITIES

Learning disabilities (LD) are by far the most common of all exceptionalities that students may exhibit. Students with learning disabilities are thought to have a variety of neurobiological conditions that affect the retrieval, processing, and/or the expression of information. It is important to note that a student who has been identified as having a learning disability has to have, by definition, normal or above-normal intelligence. In fact, some students with learning disabilities are also classified as gifted and talented. A learning disability negatively impacts a student's ability to use and/or acquire basic skills in listening, speaking, reading, writing, and/or mathematics. The most common types of learning disabilities focus on basic language and/or reading skills.

During the 2000–01 school year, 2.9 million LD students received services. Of this number, males receiving services for LD outnumbered females by three to one (U.S. Department of Education, 2002). Generally, students with learning disabilities do not outgrow their disability and there is no "cure" for learning disabilities. However, as a student matures and is remediated or gains compensatory skills (skills that allow the student to compensate for an impairment), the severity of the impairment may be reduced to the point where it is no longer a significant impediment to the student's academic achievement. A definitive cure for learning disabilities does not exist. However, with the proper support and interventions, LD students can be successful and productive in school.

As is the case with mental retardation, a variety of specific definitions exist for the term "learning disability." The two most widely used definitions are given by IDEA and the National Joint Committee on Learning Disabilities (NJCLD) (Heward, 2003). IDEA's definition focuses on the impaired ability to process spoken or written language, which may result in an imperfect ability to listen, think, speak, read, write, spell, or do mathematical calculations (Hallahan & Kauffman, 2000).

The NJCLD definition also focuses on an inability to process spoken and/or written information but differentiates a learning disability from other impairments such as social skills, mental retardation, cultural differences, and native language. The NJCLD definition also differs from IDEA's definition in that it includes adults.

In addition to these national definitions, most states and districts have three criteria that must be met for a student to be identified as LD:

- A severe discrepancy exists between the student's intellectual ability and academic achievement.
- The student's difficulties are not the result of another known condition that can create learning problems.
- A need for special education services exists (Heward, 2003).

The most important characteristic that students with learning disabilities share is that they demonstrate specific and significant achievement deficits despite having normal or even above-normal intelligence. While uncommon, it is possible for students with specific learning disabilities to also be academically gifted and talented. It is important that teachers understand that they can provide enriching activities for these students while addressing remedial activities students need at the same time.

Common Types of Learning Disabilities

Many types of disabilities have "subcategories." A number of different subcategories exist for learning disabilities. We have chosen to describe the most commonly recognized subcategories as each has unique characteristics that have a significant impact on the best instructional strategies to use with the individual student.

Dyslexia

Dyslexia is probably the best-known learning disability. Dyslexia is a condition that makes it extremely difficult for individuals with average intelligence to read, write, and spell in their native language. Dyslexia is a persistent deficit in basic reading skills that includes problems in letter recognition (Friend & Bursuck, 1996). Although dyslexia is a lifelong condition, individuals with dyslexia can respond successfully to timely and appropriate interventions. Depending on the context, these interventions can involve remedial activities such as computer-assisted reading programs or an assistive technology such as a text reader.

Dysgraphia

Like dyslexia, dysgraphia is a neurological disorder. Dysgraphia specifically involves difficulties with writing—in particular, the physical aspects of writing, spelling, or putting one's thoughts on paper. Some of the more common signs of dysgraphia are:

- Illegible handwriting
- Inconsistency in how letters and words look
- Difficulty writing within the margins or line spacing, along with inconsistent spacing between words
- Difficulty fleshing out ideas onto paper despite being able to discuss ideas verbally with ease
- Avoidance of activities involving writing

In addition to word processing, assistive technologies such as tape recorders can help a student with academic tasks such as note taking.

Dyscalculia

Dyscalculia is a learning disability involving math skills that affects about 2 to 6.5% of the elementary-school-age population (U.S. Department of Education, 2002). Dyscalculia can be quantitative, qualitative, or intermediate. Quantitative indicates a deficit in counting and calculating. Qualitative indicates a difficulty in conceptualizing math processes. Intermediate indicates the inability to work with numbers or symbols. Students identified as having dyscalculia exhibit some very interesting characteristics including:

- Normal or advanced language and other skills and often a good visual memory for the printed word
- Difficulty with math processes such as addition, subtraction, multiplication, and division
- Poor sense of direction, trouble reading maps, telling time, and grappling with mechanical processes
- The tendency to make mistakes such as number substitutions, reversals, and omissions (National Center for Learning Disabilities, 2003)

It is interesting to note that some individuals with dyscalculia have gone on to become math teachers, because while dyscalculia can interfere with rote memorization tasks such as remembering multiplication tables, it does not necessarily affect higher-order logical reasoning skills, which are needed for higher-level math such as algebra, calculus, and geometry.

GIFTED AND TALENTED STUDENTS

Gifted and talented (GT) students are very different from students with disabilities in that they excel in some human endeavor whether it be art, music, writing, math, or other intellectual pursuit. In fact, because GT students often become bored in many educational settings, they require instructional modifications that will help meet their unique learning needs but that lie outside the normal school curriculum. While some GT students are gifted across all areas of the curriculum, others demonstrate advanced skill in only one or more curricular areas and have normal functioning or even deficits in other areas.

There are many widely accepted definitions of GT. Historically, these definitions relied on measures of intelligence to identify students as GT. Current definitions of GT shift focus from IQ to environment, personality, and specific talents as the defining characteristics of GT (Heward, 2003).

Gifted and talented students tend to have common traits. Shaklee, Whitmore, Barton, Barbour, Ambross, and Viechnicki (1989) have identified characteristics that highly intelligent children often exhibit: exceptional memory, exceptional synthesis of information, exceptional application of knowledge in unique/novel situations, and exceptional motivation.

It is commonly acknowledged that creativity is one of the defining characteristics of GT students. Although many agree that creativity is easy to identify, it is not always easy to define. Guilford (1987) has identified several common characteristics of creative people including fluency (high productivity), flexibility, novelty, originality, the ability to elaborate on answers, the ability to synthesize information, the ability to analyze information, and what is commonly known as multitasking (the ability to do several things at once).

SUMMARY

As a classroom teacher, you are faced with a tremendous challenge when trying to meet the needs of all your students, especially those with diverse needs brought on by a disability or exceptionality. However, the more you understand about your students, the easier it will be for you to provide instruction that will enable your students to be successful.

The five diverse learner types identified and described in this chapter were: English Language Learners/English as a Second Language Learners, learners with physical disabilities, learners with cognitive disabilities, learners identified as learning disabled, and learners identified as gifted and talented. Students in each of these categories have a variety of unique needs that include:

- Cultural, SES, and language concerns
- Visual, hearing, and mobility impairments
- Behavioral impairments
- Information-processing impairments
- Talents that challenge the curriculum

Fortunately, these issues can be addressed through an effective combination of instructional strategies and technologies.

FOR FURTHER APPLICATION

Integrating technology into a classroom of diverse learners is a difficult process. Understanding the general characteristics of each learner is an important first step toward making an effective match among learner, technology, and instructional strategy. There are a number of resources available that can help you with this. Below is a list of various resources that can provide you with more information about diverse learners.

- The Exceptional Learners Education Web (http://www.iteachilearn .com/uh/meisgeier/) provides a number of resources for teachers working with diverse learners. In addition to articles about diverse learners, the Web site includes links to lesson plans and instructional strategies that can be used with a wide variety of students. The home page includes several links to papers about using technology with diverse learners.

- Online communication can be a valuable tool for solving problems encountered when working with diverse learners. Teachers.Net (http:// teachers.net/) provides links to several discussion boards on diverse learners including ELL students and students with learning disabilities. It also provides links to lesson plans and other materials developed by teachers and to resources that will help you better utilize technology in the classroom.

- In addition to online resources, many books and other print media are available online. One Web site, full of excellent online resources, is IDEA Practices (http://www.ideapractices.org/index.php). As well as resources about exceptional learners, IDEA Practices has several links to resources that will help you better integrate technology into a diverse classroom.

- Professional development opportunities are another way of learning more about diverse learners. Many of these workshops or institutes are national in scope. The Web site of the Lawrence Hall of Science at the University of California, Berkeley (http://www.lawrencehallofscience .org/profdev/), provides information about summer institutes that can help you meet the needs of diverse learners.

3 Diverse Learners and Innovative Technologies

Chapter Guiding Questions

This chapter will help you answer the following questions:

- How is the term "technology" defined?
- What is the difference between assistive/adaptive technology and learning support technology?
- What are examples of assistive/adaptive technologies?
- What are examples of learning support technologies?
- What are examples of extension technologies (i.e., innovative technologies used to support and challenge gifted and talented students)?

Currently, the word "technology" is most often used to refer to computers and computing tools, but it is really much more than that. Technology can be defined as the practical application of scientific learning. For example, scientists perform research on how electricity works, and engineers apply this knowledge in useful ways; the useful application (like electric lights or radios) is the technology. We use the term "innovative technology" to indicate something that is relatively new. Computing technologies are relatively new; so are many video-based and telephone technologies.

In this chapter, we will describe the innovative technologies that may be particularly beneficial to diverse learners. While the focus is on computer hardware and software, we also will describe other technologies that are particularly helpful to persons with disabilities. Technologies to support diverse learners can be divided into two broad categories: *assistive/adaptive* and *learning support* (or *supportive*).

Assistive/adaptive technologies help a person with common tasks or make something physically accessible that would be inaccessible otherwise. Assistive/adaptive technologies do not promote learning per se, nor do they address any specific curriculum. Assistive/adaptive technologies are "content-free" technologies that allow an individual to function in a situation that because of an individual difference might be otherwise impossible.

Learning support or supportive technologies directly address issues of learning and the curriculum. Supportive technologies can assist a learner through remediation, compensation (alternative cognitive tools), or extension (opportunities for greater exploration).

ASSISTIVE/ADAPTIVE TECHNOLOGIES

Assistive devices include any device that individuals with disabilities might use to help them learn and function more effectively. By current estimates, more than four thousand assistive technologies have been designed for students and teachers. These devices are everything from wheelchairs to a wide assortment of high-tech tools, including:

- Hearing aids and amplification devices that enable hearing-impaired students to hear what occurs in the classroom
- Glare-reduction screens, screen magnifiers, and Braille note-taking devices that enable visually impaired students to participate more fully
- Voice-recognition software that turns the spoken word into type on a computer screen so students with physical impairments can write
- Technologies that enable students with severe disabilities to control their computers simply by following letters and commands on the computer screen with their eyes (Steele-Carlin, 2001)

Computers are increasingly significant as assistive technology devices because they can be modified to support a wide variety of diverse learners. Specialized hardware can provide increased access for differently abled learners. Specialized software can help compensate for cognitive and/or perceptual impairments as well as provide assistance for English Language Learners.

Hardware

Hardware is any part of a computing system that can be regularly handled by a person. The box that contains the computer is hardware, as are the electronic components in the box. A monitor is hardware. Cables that connect devices are hardware (as are the devices themselves).

A computer is a hardware device that digitally processes information. Over the past few decades computers have evolved from gigantic contraptions taking up entire buildings to "mainframes" that take up the space of a large room, to "desktop" devices the size of a small storage box, to laptop and handheld devices that travel easily (some fitting into a coat pocket). Smaller computers, "laptop" or "notebook" sized, can be particularly useful to students for note taking and writing.

Input/Output devices are specialized hardware that allows the user to send and receive messages from the computer itself. A monitor is an output device: it provides a visual interpretation of the computer actions. A printer is another type of output device. A keyboard is an input device: it allows a user to send messages to the computer. A mouse is another common input device.

Computer Input Devices

Input devices can be constructed to accommodate a wide range of abilities. *Keyboards* and *mice* are two of the most common computer input devices. These can be modified to accommodate diverse individuals. Figure 3.1 is a picture of the BigKeys Keyboard (Greystone Digital, Inc., 2002), which has extra large keys to facilitate locating and pressing the keys correctly.

Figure 3.1   A BigKeys Keyboard

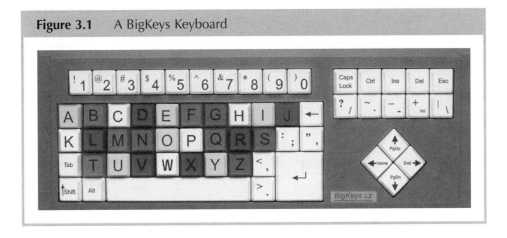

SOURCE: Courtesy of Greystone Digital, Inc. BigKeys, BigKeys Plus, and BigKeys LX are exclusive trademarks of Greystone Digital, Inc.

Another example of an alternate keyboard is *IntelliKeys*, which is a programmable alternative keyboard that plugs into any Macintosh or Windows computer. It enables students with physical, visual, or cognitive disabilities (such as CP, spina bifida, blindness, or dysgraphia) to easily type, enter numbers, navigate on-screen displays, and execute menu commands (IntelliTools, 2003a).

Many people have trouble manipulating a standard computer mouse; a *trackball* can be a very good alternative. A trackball is basically an upside-down mouse with a much larger rolling ball that requires a great deal less hand movement. As with adaptive keyboards, trackballs and other input devices can help students with impairments such as CP and spinal cord injuries input text.

A variety of other input devices exist that some individuals may find easier to use than either a keyboard or a mouse. *Touch screens* can be used to provide a direct one-to-one correlation between input and output. A touch screen is a specific type of monitor that lets the user provide input by direct touch (monitors are specially built for this purpose; there are also touch screen add-on kits available that can transform a standard monitor into a touch screen). Tablet devices provide yet another form of input. A tablet device is a pressure-sensitive pad that sends messages to the computer when the user presses on the pad using a stylus or finger.

Traditional keyboard and mouse devices can be redesigned, modified, or adapted to accommodate a wide variety of users with specific needs. In addition to students with physical impairments, students with cognitive impairments such as mental retardation, autism, and learning disabilities can benefit from these adaptations. Examples of general adaptations include:

Sequential Keystroke Input. Software programs can be loaded that allow the user to enter keystrokes sequentially that others enter simultaneously and still achieve the same effect. For example, the Ctrl, Alt, and Delete keys are all held down together to perform a soft reboot on a PC. With this program running, Ctrl is pressed, then Alt is pressed, then Delete is pressed and a soft reboot still occurs.

Key Repeat Rate Control. Programs exist that allow the PC user to adjust the key repeat speed of the keyboard or completely turn off the keystroke repeat function.

Keyboard Macros. Software and hardware solutions exist to allow a few keystrokes to be automatically translated into multiple keystrokes. Macros reduce the number of keystrokes needed to generate a word, phrase, or paragraph. For example, an individual's initials can be used to generate the entire signature block on the screen.

Alternative Keyboards. Several alternative keyboards exist that may be more easily used by various individuals with mobility impairments. There are small versions of keyboards and large, expanded keyboards. There are also keyboards that are not physically connected to the PC they control, but rely on infrared transmission to a receiver attached to the PC. The standard keyboard can also be remapped to be used as a right-handed or left-handed Dvorak keyboard for a person who types with a single hand.

Keyboard Enhancements. A raised dot (a bleb) or a Braille marker can be added to the standard keycaps on selected keys such as the home row keys, Ctrl, or Alt to provide tactile keyboard orientation. In addition, auditory status indicators for toggle keys, such as Shift Lock or Num Lock, can often be provided by software. Other keyboard aids include adhesive-backed keycap labels that can be purchased and applied to the standard keyboard that have large, bold letters. These labels are available in either white-on-black background or black-on-white background.

Non-Keyboard-Dependent Input Devices. A variety of alternative input devices allow keystrokes to be generated by various mechanisms and then transmitted as if generated by the keyboard. Examples are sip and puff systems, muscle switches, optical pointer devices, Morse code input systems, and eye scanning systems. As with alternate input devices, these devices are well suited for students with physical impairments such as paralysis and CP.

Word Prediction Packages. Word prediction packages may be used in conjunction with many PC application packages, keyboard enhancement products, and alternative input mechanisms. Word prediction packages try to anticipate the next word the user will be typing and display a list of choices. If the word desired is not on the list, the user selects the first character of the word and the selection list changes. Word prediction can significantly reduce the number of keystrokes the user must enter from either a keyboard or an alternative input device. Some packages will change the listing of words predicted based on past usage. Others have a set listing of selections and a predefined presentation order.

Speech Recognition. Many individuals who are unable to access the keyboard at all or have very limited access to the keyboard can successfully use speech input. Speech recognition may be used to either supplement or replace the use of a keyboard.

Robotic Devices. Voice-activated robotic arm devices can be used in conjunction with a workstation. These units provide persons with severe mobility impairments with voice control of the computer and a robotic arm to perform tasks such as loading diskettes, turning pages in a book, and answering the phone. Other environmental control systems may also be attached to this system to control the lights, blinds, and other things in the room.

Mouse Alternatives. For programs dependent on mouse functions, keyboard commands often can provide equivalent functions. The use of a trackball, which allows the user to make very small motions to move the curser, may also be a viable alternative to the large sweeping motions often needed for effective utilization of a mouse.

Keyguard. A keyguard is a smooth-surfaced template with holes corresponding to key locations. The keyguard is placed over a standard keyboard and promotes keyboard accuracy by stabilizing hand movements and preventing inadvertent multiple keystrokes.

Hands-Free Control. A specific example of a hands-free control device is the Smart-Nav AT cursor control system. This assistive technology is particularly helpful to people who require a hands-free mouse alternative (e.g., persons with amyotrophic lateral sclerosis [ALS] or spinal cord injuries). The Smart-Nav AT accommodates a number of computer interface navigation alternatives including head tracking, dwell clicking, switch clicking, and on-screen virtual keyboard software (Assistive Technologies, Inc., 2002).

Another example of a device that allows hands-free control is the Magic Wand Keyboard. This miniature computer keyboard with a built-in mouse allows anyone who has limited or no hand/arm movement to fully access any IBM or Apple Macintosh computer. It requires no strength and works with the touch of a wand (handheld or mouthstick). Using only the slightest hand or head motion, the keyboard allows people with disabilities easy access to a computer system (In Touch Systems, 2003).

Eye Movement Activation Switch. Another example of a highly specialized, hands-free input device is the SCATIR (Self-Calibrating Auditory Tone Infrared) Switch. This device allows a person with very limited mobility to control computer/devices with eye movement. The SCATIR Switch is an experimental multipurpose momentary-contact optical switch with auditory feedback designed for use by persons who experience difficulty in activating mechanical switches. It works by detecting a beam of reflected pulsed infrared light. It is suitable for use with a variety of control gestures, including eyeblink, eyebrow movement, finger movement, head movement, and facial muscle movement. Because it works on an optical principle, it can be activated at a distance (Michigan State University Artificial Language Laboratory, 2002).

Computer Output Devices

Just as input devices can help make computers more accessible to people with disabilities, assistive/adaptive output devices can help make computer output more understandable and useful. Traditional output devices include monitors (TV-like screens commonly used to see files as one works on them, view video, view e-mail, and browse the World Wide Web) and printers (devices that produce output on paper). Like input devices, output devices can be modified to better serve the needs of people with disabilities. For example, building in *Visual Redundancy* in the output system of any device helps to ensure that important information conveyed by beeps or speech during computer-related tasks are also displayed visually for the user unable to detect the auditory information. Students classified as deaf or hard of hearing can benefit from these devices. Examples of assistive/adaptive output hardware include "low vision" accommodations, modified display of hard copy material, captioning, tactile output, and speech synthesizers. These devices are especially helpful for students classified as legally or educationally blind.

"Low Vision" Accommodations. These devices assist people with visual impairments. They include: *glare protection screens* (to minimize visual fatigue associated with glare on the monitor) and *large monitors with high resolution* (19-inch to 25-inch screens allow for increased character size in proportion to monitor dimensions and provide a crisp, sharp image).

Modified Display of Hard Copy Material. Hardware that will magnify any item placed under a closed-circuit television (CCTV) camera can be used to create a modified display. Documents, drawings, phone messages, and so forth, can be seen enlarged on a CCTV monitor. An inexpensive alternative to specialized output hardware can be a standard copy machine with enlarging and reducing capability. Copy machines provide enlarged-print copies for persons with impaired vision who find magnification helpful and small-print copies for persons with visual impairments such as tunnel vision, which restricts the field of view.

Captioning. Captioned video output provides the text equivalent of sounds and speech as they occur on the video. Captioning display is rapidly becoming a standard option on commercial digital video discs (DVDs).

Tactile Output. Tactile output such as raised line drawings may be useful for some individuals who are blind. Several Braille printers and wax jet printers have the capability of producing raised line drawings. There are also handheld devices that use an array of vibrating pins to present a tactile outline of the characters or text under the viewing window of the device.

Speech Synthesizers. These devices are used in conjunction with a screen reader to convert screen contents into spoken words using synthetic speech (a variety of voices are currently available, the most natural sounding are arguably the male "Bruce" and the female "Agnes"). Synthesized speech is still at a point in its development where the output does not sound natural. However, it is at a point where it can be used as a reliable output method, and continuing improvements in text-to-speech software show great promise in creating a natural-sounding voice output.

Internet-Based Communication

Internet-based communication (computers networked using the common TCP/IP protocol) is an inexpensive and generally reliable method of local, regional, and long-distance communication. E-mail and Web browsing are the most common forms of communication. Telephone systems have developed a great deal, creating a variety of new communication options as well.

E-mail is similar to sending and receiving letters or memos. For students with limited mobility, e-mail can be a very good means of communicating with others. It can be a particularly good opportunity for students who may have to participate in classes while staying at home. E-mail is text based; but unlike printed letters, most people using e-mail are very forgiving of typographical and grammar errors (because the aim of the medium is most often to write short messages quickly). Conversely, since e-mail is an "asynchronous" (not time-specific) method of communication, individuals who may need some time to create even a brief message can comfortably take the time they need without breaking the natural flow of the messages. In other words, it's much less likely that a person communicating via e-mail will recognize that one or more members of the conversation have an impairment, or use a different means of inputting or outputting information.

A teacher may want to create a *buddy list* of e-mail addresses of people interested in communicating via e-mail with students. These people may be fellow students, parents, teachers, and/or professionals willing to share information about their work or hobbies.

Students may also communicate using Instant Messenger (IM) service (e.g., *AOL Instant Messenger, MSN Messenger,* or ICQ). This is similar to e-mail in that it is primarily short, text-based messages sent and received. The big difference is that IM is a synchronous mode of communication; therefore, the time it takes to create and respond to messages becomes more of a factor in successfully corresponding.

Internet-Based Video and Audio. Students with limited mobility who may need to attend school from home can also talk directly with teachers and classmates through their computer via two-way audio/video. Popular programs for this purpose include *NetMeeting* (Microsoft, 2002) and *iVisit* (iVisit, 2003). If students have a computer connected to the Internet, these programs can be an inexpensive and effective means of communication. Students need to own a Web cam, and their computer needs to have appropriate audio/video cards installed. The software necessary to communicate via audio/video can be obtained for free.

Telephone Systems (Telephony)

While telephones themselves are not a new technology, there have been a number of improvements and adaptations to telephone systems that support a diverse population. The newest telephony technologies have the potential to convert text to speech and speech to text to allow communication between text-based and auditory mediums.

Teletypewriter (TTY) devices, such as the one from Deafworks, use standard land lines to transmit typed information via small, telephone handset devices, allowing people with hearing impairments to use the telephone effectively. Two persons with TTY devices can communicate directly, and the federal government requires each state to have a relay service for persons with a TTY device (Hallahan & Kauffman, 2000).

The most recent advancements in digital cell phone technology open up new worlds for persons with hearing impairments. Digital cell phones offer text messaging between cell phones as well as e-mail plans. Other examples of assistive/adaptive telephone hardware include:

Speaker Phone. For individuals unable to easily pick up or hold a telephone handset, a speaker phone may be quite useful.

Gooseneck Receiver Holder. For individuals in a setting where a speaker phone would not be appropriate, a flexible gooseneck arm with a clamp to hold the phone receiver may be useful. Typically, a small device is used in the handset cradle to perform the "off-hook" or "hang-up" function that happens when the handset is physically placed in the handset cradle.

Phone Headset. Some individuals may prefer to use a phone headset that is worn on the head with a small microphone positioned in front of the mouth. However, it must be pointed out that individuals who are unable to put on and remove the headset independently might perceive this as decreasing their independent movement.

Speed Dialing. Many phone systems offer enhancements that allow a short one- or two-digit code to be used to dial a number. For an individual who has difficulty dialing, this can be quite helpful. Some phone sets can also be purchased that have a speed dial feature built into the phone set itself. A few of these devices also accommodate voice-activated speed dialing (U.S. Department of Energy, 2003a).

Hearing-Aid-Compatible Phones. When a person wearing a hearing aid attempts to use a telephone that is not hearing aid compatible, they often hear a very loud, high-pitched squeal similar to the sound heard when a public address system exhibits a microphone feedback problem. This can be quite uncomfortable and prevents people from using the telephone to carry on a conversation. Individuals with hearing aids should have access to hearing-aid-compatible phones. The Hearing Aid Compatibility Act (Public Law 100394) required that by August 1989 all essential telephones and all telephones manufactured in the United States or imported "provide internal means for effective use with hearing aids that are designed to be compatible with telephones which meet established technical standards for hearing aid compatibility." Some individuals who wear hearing aids may also need an additional phone amplification device.

Amplification. For individuals with hearing impairments, there are several methods of amplifying the speech being heard over a telephone. There are devices designed for people who use a hearing aid and for those who do not. Battery-powered, portable handset amplifiers are available with telephones that are not normally set up for use by a hearing-impaired individual.

Hearing Aids

Like the telephone, hearing aids are not a new technology. However, the more modern designs are smaller and more effective than ever before. The two most common types fit either behind the ear or farther down the hearing canal (Hallahan & Kauffman, 2000). The behind-the-ear type is most powerful and so most commonly used.

Another hearing aid used commonly in the classroom is the FM Listening System. The system is structured so that the teacher wears a microphone into which he or she can speak normally; the sound is then broadcast to the student's hearing aid (American Hearing Aid Associates, 2002).

Augmentative and Alternative Communication (AAC) Devices

Augmentative and alternative communication includes any manual or electronic means by which a person ". . . expresses wants and needs, shares information, engages in social closeness, or manages social etiquette" (Franklin & Beukelman, 1991, as cited in Hallahan & Kauffman, 2000).

AAC devices enhance a person's ability to interact. A simple version of an AAC is a pencil and paper for a person who cannot speak. Electronic AAC devices can produce text and/or synthesized speech through a variety of input options. Some electronic AAC devices are used as input devices for a generic computer; others have computing capabilities built in (these are often smaller, portable devices). An example is the AlphaSmart (AlphaSmart, Inc., 2003), a portable keyboard system that travels easily and can be networked to more common computers.

Software

Software is the set of instructions created by an author that causes the computer to produce specific outputs based on specific inputs. Software is different from hardware in that it cannot actually be handled in the same way hardware can (e.g., the CD-ROM that contains a software program is hardware; the program on that CD-ROM is a set of instructions that the computer can execute). Software can be transmitted from one digital device to another (this is referred to as "uploading" or "downloading") by the immediate duplication of the set of instructions.

Unlike hardware, software can be replicated and distributed pretty much infinitely. However, one must keep in mind the legal restrictions that limit the number of copies a person may make or use of any program. Software can be classified into three categories:

- *Commercial.* Any software that the user purchases a license to use. The license may allow the use of the software on just one computer or a specified number of computers, or it may apply to all the computers owned by an institution.

- *Shareware.* Any software that is made available to the general public with the expectation that anyone who makes regular use of it will pay a fee to its creator. The fees are generally low (well under $100).

- *Freeware.* Any software that is made available to the general public free of charge. These are often smaller software packages that perform a specific function or facilitate the use of a specific piece of hardware (e.g., manufacturers of printers often supply freeware that allows their product to connect to a personal computer).

Assistive/adaptive software falls into two broad categories: *translation* and *enhancement*. Translation software is anything that converts the input or output from one communication mode to another (e.g., changing from English to Spanish or changing from visual output to audio).

Enhancement software does not change the mode of communication; it supports that mode by offering a greater range of output options (e.g., increasing the volume of a sound file or enlarging text).

Translation Software

Software can convert text and the spoken word in a wide variety of ways. Text can become audible, the spoken word can become visible, and one language can be translated into another. As with all translation devices (including human beings), some are more reliable than others. Although experts have been working with and developing translation software for decades, it is still very much in its infancy in terms of reliability. Translating anything from one mode to another is difficult for anyone; creating software that reliably does this job is even more difficult.

Text-to-speech software converts the printed word into the spoken word. While this software continues to improve with each new version, at present the resulting synthesized speech does not sound completely natural. A popular example is the speech synthesizer that physicist Stephen Hawking uses; there is no mistaking this synthesized voice for a human one, although it does have a definite male sound to it.

An example of a readily available version is the Macintosh OS X operating system, which has text-to-speech translation software built into it (one can choose a specific keyboard key, then any highlighted text in any program will be translated into synthesized speech when that key is pressed). The program *HyperStudio*, which is popular among elementary-age students and their teachers, also has a built-in text-to-speech translation program called *Blabbermouth*. Programs such as *Text to Speech Software* (Text to Speech Software.Com, 2002) can be used to read back text. The output file can be stored on the computer or can be saved in MP3 format for downloading into a portable player.

Students with some types of physical or cognitive impairments and students with communication disorders may find text-to-speech software particularly useful. Using a device like the Kurzweil Omni 1000, a student can convert the printed word into synthesized speech (Kurzweil, 1996, as cited in Hallahan & Kauffman, 2000).

The most popular screen reader worldwide, *JAWS for Windows*, works with a PC to provide access to software applications and the Internet. With its internal software speech synthesizer and the computer's sound card, information from the screen is read aloud, providing technology to access a wide variety of information, education, and job-related applications. *JAWS* also outputs to refreshable Braille displays, providing Braille support for any screen reader (Freedom Scientific, 2003).

Like text-to-speech, *speech-to-text* software is still very much in its developmental stages, but great strides have been made in recent years. Programs like IBM's *ViaVoice* (IBM Corporation, 2003b) offer practical and relatively inexpensive speech-to-text capabilities. Generally, one needs to "train" this type of software to accurately recognize a specific user. This is accomplished by reading about twenty minutes' worth of text into a microphone connected to the computer running the software. The user can provide corrective feedback to the software as part of its "training." The more an individual uses the software, the better the software is able to translate speech to text.

The same principles used to create speech-to-text software are applied to "voice recognition" programs. The programs are a variant on speech-to-text that allows the user to issue voice commands to a computer (e.g., "open file," "launch application," or "shut down").

Another type of speech-to-text situation is "closed captioning." This is not actually a software program as much as it is a selectable option with some software—particularly digital video disc (DVD) formats. DVDs often have a closed-captioning option—that is, the DVD allows the user to choose a variation of the video presentation that includes subtitles (often DVDs offer a variety of subtitle languages, as well as the option to present the movie in more than one spoken language).

Optical Character Recognition (OCR). Using OCR software to convert or "translate" printed documents to a text file may be quite useful. Many individuals with mobility impairments are able to read a document on the PC with greater ease than handling a printed version of the document. Braille translation software can be used to translate traditional text documents to Braille (Braille has its own spelling and grammar rules). Printers such as one from Enabling Technologies (2003) can be used to print the document.

Language Translation. The term "assistive technology" is not entirely accurate with ELL students because they do not have a disability. However, several technologies exist that can assist ELL students by facilitating access to English language materials. For example, a number of translation software programs are available via the World Wide Web. These sites generally require the user to type in (or cut and paste) text in one language, then choose the language they would like to output. The more popular languages available for translation include English, French, Spanish, German, Dutch, Norwegian, and Portuguese. Translation software for Chinese, Korean, and Japanese is also available, but it requires that the computer have specialized software for these text characters. Examples of Web-based translation programs include Freetranslation.com (SDL International, 2003) and Alta Vista's Babelfish component (AltaVista, 2003).

Web-based translators are also available that will translate the content of an entire Web page or site: the user types the URL (the Web address) into a form field, then selects the language to translate and clicks on a link with the term "translate" (or something similar). The Web site is then displayed with its original design (graphics, etc.) but translated into the requested language. Software companies like Babelfish (AltaVista, 2003) and InterTran (Translation Experts Limited, 2003) specialize in this type of translation.

IBM offers several Web readers that speak the text of Web sites back to the user (IBM Corporation, 2003a). Along with English versions of their software, they also offer Web readers in several languages other than English including Spanish and French. These Web readers will read an English Web site back to the user in the language selected. Thus, ESL students whose native language is Spanish can have an English Web site read back to them in Spanish. One noticeable problem with this software is that words are read in the order that they appear in English; thus, the spoken output does not sound entirely natural in the translated language.

Enhancement Software

Enhancement software is any program that allows the user to intensify the output. This does not change the output mode (it does not perform a translation); it changes the magnitude of the output. A relatively simple example is volume control: most recent-model computing devices allow a user to increase or decrease the volume of the sound output (on a Macintosh computer, there are designated sound increase/decrease keys on the keyboard).

Magnification. Students with low vision can use software to magnify screen contents. Microsoft and Apple have magnification functions built into their respective Windows and Macintosh operating systems. Software and hardware solutions exist to present the images on the computer in a larger format. Text character size can be increased up to 216 times. Several software packages are available that will print large, bold text with either a dot matrix or a laser printer.

SUPPORTIVE TECHNOLOGIES

Unlike assistive/adaptive technologies, which may be helpful in a wide variety of situations outside the classroom, supportive technologies directly address issues of learning and the curriculum. Supportive technologies can provide extra help in three ways: remediation, compensation (alternative cognitive tools), or extension (opportunities for greater exploration).

REMEDIATION TECHNOLOGIES

Many software programs are available to help with remediation in a variety of areas. Online resources such as Riverdeep (Riverdeep Interactive Learning Limited, 2003) provide ways to search for and purchase software programs.

"Drill and skill" software like *Reader Rabbit* (Broderbund, 2001) offer opportunities for students struggling with specific content to practice on their own or with the help of a teacher, teaching assistant, or parent. Another example is *IntelliTools Math,* a software program developed under a grant from the National Science Foundation. Designed to reinforce essential math skills for all students, *IntelliTools Math* offers the teacher a means to easily create specialized math activities, with access features for students with different learning abilities (IntelliTools, 2003b). MathPad Plus electronic worksheets (see Figure 3.2) are also distributed by IntelliTools. They are designed specifically to facilitate working with fractions and decimals.

One thing to keep in mind is the importance of finding software that offers the appropriate remediation while presenting everything in an age-appropriate manner. A student may benefit from the skills covered in *Reader Rabbit* but may rebel against participation if he or she perceives the presentation to be "babyish." On the other hand, something that might not be considered age appropriate for a specific student when it is presented in printed format may be perfectly acceptable when presented on a computer (e.g., the book *Arthur's Teacher Trouble* may be seen as a "kid's book" to a thirteen-year-old, but the same content may be completely acceptable when viewed on the computer as a *Living Book).*

Many programs have historically come on CD-ROM to be installed on a local computer. With the Internet, more services are coming available in a subscription format (Riverdeep is one example), allowing the teacher to pick and choose modules that are customizable for students' needs.

In addition to reading, writing, and other remedial programs, *life skills software* can be very useful, especially for students with mental retardation or autism. Life skills software ranges from simple, everyday activities (e.g., telling time or using money) to more complex social interactions (e.g., conflict resolution or choosing a career).

Figure 3.2 A MathPad Plus Electronic Worksheet

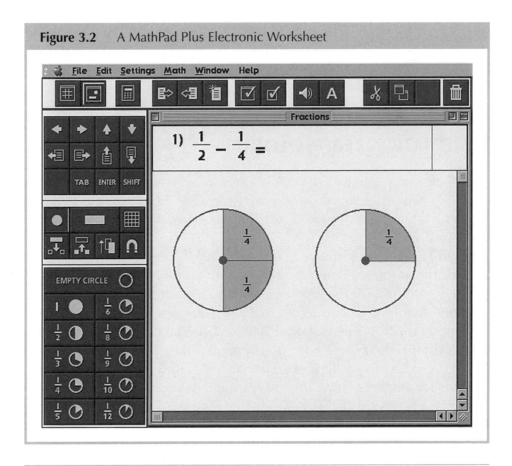

SOURCE: Used with permission of IntelliTools, Inc.

For Students With Behavioral Impairments

Although not a remediation technology per se, a number of online resources for students with behavioral impairments can help with remediation activity in this area. One example is the Center for Effective Collaboration and Practice (2003), which provides a large number of resources for teachers who have students with emotional impairments in their classroom.

COMPENSATORY TECHNOLOGIES

Compensatory technologies provide cognitive tools that students can use to accomplish school-related assignments and activities. Word processing as a writing tool is one of the best examples. Students can readily engage in the writing process while freed from things such as letter formation and in some cases spelling (using spell-checking software). Students can also save work as a digital file, therefore bypassing traditional steps of recopying work with each new draft.

Compensatory technologies often require students to learn a good deal about new technologies in order to make the best use of them. For example, students need to learn how to keyboard, save their work (which also means understanding the file or directory structure of the computing environment), and print out a hard copy.

Recent advances in computer technology have much to offer students with learning disabilities, both as tools for instruction in school and as tools for life that can be used to compensate for specific impairments. For years, teachers of students with learning disabilities have searched for means to help students compensate for their inability to master certain skills. Despite adequate cognitive ability, students with learning disabilities have difficulties with basic skills such as reading and writing, which can prevent full participation in the classroom and later in critical adult life activities. Computer technology provides the answer for many of these students. A student with dysgraphia (i.e., inability to produce legible handwriting) can use a computer with a word-processing program to alleviate much of this problem. Students with severe problems in spelling can functionally compensate using spell checkers and online thesauruses. Word prediction programs that can anticipate words from a few letters can increase both accuracy and speed of input. Students who have severe reading problems can use a computer in much the same way students with visual impairment do through enlarged print size or text-to-speech.

Computer technology can provide the kind of drill and practice that many students with learning disabilities need to help them develop fluency in such areas as mathematics facts and reading decoding. Additionally, software programs provide the multisensory and interactive experiences that can be so important for students who are easily distracted. Another kind of software that can help students with writing problems is organizational software. These programs help users through processes such as outlining and concept mapping. Although not necessarily developed for students with learning disabilities, the programs can be very helpful for students who have difficulty organizing and synthesizing information (Southwest Educational Development Laboratory, 2003).

Calculators

Calculators are a type of compensatory technology. They can be used for simpler math functions (addition, subtraction, multiplication, and division), allowing students to focus on more advanced math content.

Making Developmentally Appropriate Material More Engaging to Learners

Teachers can use computing tools to present developmentally appropriate materials in an age-appropriate manner. Developing slide-show presentations using software like *PowerPoint* lets the teacher choose appropriate language, type size, and graphics. Organizing information using Web development tools (creating a Web site that exists only on a local computer, or a "Web Quest" on the World Wide Web) allows students to explore various aspects of the content in their own way. Offering alternate representations of classroom content can be very important for diverse students, and engagement is always crucial in setting up successful learning environments. Multimedia with still images, moving images, and audio can go a long way to help engage students.

Students can create their own materials as well. Digital cameras, scanners, and microphones give students an opportunity to input their own ideas. Authoring software (like *HyperStudio* or *PowerPoint*) and Web development tools (like *Dreamweaver* or even just a simple word-processing tool like *Notepad*) allow students to create exciting presentations on any content imaginable.

EXTENSION TECHNOLOGIES

Extension technologies support students who are gifted and talented in a particular content area, giving these students greater opportunities to explore a subject. For gifted and talented students, "drill and practice" software is often *not* helpful. Students may toy with this type of software, testing to see how quickly they can complete the drills, or they may "repurpose" activities they find dull (e.g., turning "drill and skill" software into a kind of musical instrument by activating its response sounds). These students need opportunities to explore content at their own speed and the chance to form new and different connections with other content areas.

The World Wide Web is an excellent example of an opportunity to make new and unusual connections among content areas. The Web is also a good place to begin exploring research concepts using search engines and indexes (e.g., *Ask Jeeves for Kids* or *Yahooligans*).

Gifted and talented students may find personally created materials, like those mentioned in the Compensatory Technologies section, a challenging and rewarding experience. Creating digital video, multimedia presentations, and/or Web sites can ground the deeper exploration of content in a practical and fun activity.

MOOs and MUDs

MOOs and MUDs are computer-based communication activities in which individuals participate in a shared virtual world. This kind of activity can be an exciting Language Arts and Literature extension. A number of MUDs and MOOs exist that allow participants to engage in the shared creation of stories set in popular science fiction and fantasy settings—like the Starfleet Academy or Middle Earth.

As with any activity that makes use of online communication with people outside the school setting, some caution must be taken to avoid placing students at risk. Participation in public MOO or MUD activity should be carefully monitored by a trusted adult.

Programming and Robotics

Gifted and talented students may benefit from treating the computer as a medium more than as a reception device (i.e., students may gain more from creating their own presentations than merely watching or listening to professionally developed presentations). Software that facilitates programming the computer like *HyperStudio, IntelliPics, MicroWorlds Logo*, or *StageCast Creator* may be of particular interest to students who wish to explore some combination of computing environments, multimedia, and human-computer interaction. Lego produces the particularly engaging *MindStorms* package that combines essentials of programming with Lego parts that allows students to explore robotics.

SUMMARY

In Chapter 3, we explored the various technologies that may be used to support and enrich the education of diverse students. These technologies can be divided into two categories: *assistive/adaptive* and *supportive.*

Assistive/adaptive technologies include hardware that facilitates input of information into a computer and facilitates interpreting a computer's output. Examples include modified keyboards, trackballs, and AAC (augmentative alternative communication) devices.

Assistive/adaptive technologies also include software that provides support through either translation or enhancement. Some examples of translation software include text-to-speech, speech-to-text, and language translation. Enhancement software includes that which enlarges the output of a screen (magnification).

Supportive technologies can be divided into three subcategories: *remediation, compensatory,* and *extension.* Remediation includes "drill and practice" software. Compensatory includes word processors, calculators, and presentation software that can be used to present developmentally appropriate content in an age-appropriate manner. Extension includes the World Wide Web as an opportunity to make new and different connections among content areas, MOOs and MUDs, opportunities to program the computer, and robotics.

FOR FURTHER APPLICATION

Assistive/adaptive technologies can be fun for those of us who enjoy a new "toy." They are also fun in that they can open doors for students who have been limited by an impairment. They can also be challenging precisely because they require some technical skill to operate. A number of resources are available that can help you meet this challenge and integrate these new "toys" into the classroom. The three Web sites below are good starting points for a wide range of information about assistive and adaptive technology including materials and professional development opportunities.

• The Rehabilitation Engineering and Assistive Technology Society of North America (http://www.resna.org/) provides teachers with a wealth of information about assistive and adaptive technologies. In addition to print and online materials, the society sponsors an annual conference and offers certification in the area of assistive and adaptive technologies.

• The Center for Assistive Technology (http://cat.buffalo.edu/) is housed at the University at Buffalo in the School of Public Health and Health Professions. The center provides several workshops about assistive technologies as well as numerous print and online resources. The center also offers certificates in Assistive and Rehabilitation Technology and even a Ph.D. in Rehabilitation Science.

• The Center for Applied Special Technology (CAST) (http://www.cast.org) specializes in researching and developing new technologies that expand opportunities for everyone, especially persons with disabilities. CAST works closely with the U.S. Department of Education on the adoption of curricular standards that can help meet the needs of persons with disabilities. The center is also responsible for the development of many assistive technologies such as the *CAST eReader* and *Bobby*.

4 Curriculum, Technology, and Diverse Learners

Chapter Guiding Questions

This chapter will help you answer the following questions:

- What is differentiated instruction?
- What is inclusion?
- How can assistive technologies be best used in an inclusive classroom?
- How can differentiated instruction be teamed with technology to meet the needs of ELL students?
- How can teachers use technology to help them address issues of gender in the classroom?
- How can assistive technologies be included in children's IEPs to help better meet their educational needs?

Diverse learners require unique instruction that helps meet their unique learning needs. Combine this with relatively limited technological resources in the typical classroom, and the tools for planning for technology in the classroom become just as, or even more than, important as the actual technological tools themselves. The purpose of this chapter is to provide you with the instructional planning tools that can help you not only plan for technology but also integrate technology into an inclusive classroom. To do this, we will begin by introducing the concept of differentiated instruction and how differentiated instruction works. We will also discuss the inclusive classroom, what it is, and its implications for the classroom teacher. Then we will look at how different technologies can be used with different types of curricular content including English, math, science, and social studies. Along the way we will provide you with scenarios describing how a teacher can combine differentiated instruction with technology to meet the needs of a diverse population of learners. While these scenarios will provide you with a picture of what is happening in the classroom, they are also written so that they can be adapted to a variety of needs and situations.

In this chapter, we will also focus on the use of technology to meet the needs of the student with regard to higher-order thinking skills. These skills are often more complex situations requiring more planning and intervention as opposed to remedial situations in which computer software provides a highly structured instructional framework for the student.

DIFFERENTIATED INSTRUCTION: WHAT IS IT AND HOW DOES IT WORK?

A well-researched and effective instructional technique that can help the classroom teacher meet these unique needs is differentiated instruction. Differentiated instruction differs from individualized instruction in that it provides learners with more options for learning while ensuring that the classroom workload remains manageable. A teacher creates this balance by looking at similarities as well as differences among students in the classroom. By grouping students together and then dealing with the unique instructional needs of that group, the teacher can strike a balance between meeting the needs of a variety of learners with different abilities and experiences and the reality of the classroom, where one teacher is expected to work with as many as thirty students. Another advantage of differentiated instruction is that it can effectively utilize the wide variety of assistive/adaptive technologies presented in Chapter 3.

At this point, you may be asking why we are discussing differentiated instruction in a book about technology in the classroom. Differentiated instruction is uniquely suited for not only dealing with the unique learning characteristics of a wide variety of students but for also allowing the teacher to more effectively integrate limited technology resources into the day-to-day activities of the classroom. In order for technology to be most effective, it must be fully integrated into the classroom. Unfortunately, very few teachers have a classroom full of computers or a laptop for every student, so an instructional technique that both meets the unique instructional needs of each student and provides accessibility to the technology is important, and differentiated instruction does this well. If you are interested in learning more about differentiated instruction, several books on this topic are listed in the References. Differentiated instruction can be thought of as a way of teaching that provides the student with many ways to access, process, and output information that best meets their instructional needs. In a differentiated classroom, the teacher assesses the student's instructional needs, creates and/or uses instructional techniques that meet those needs, then reassesses the student's needs to inform the next round of instruction. Carol Tomlinson (2001) describes the key characteristics that form the core of a differentiated classroom. The first of these is proactive instruction in which the teacher is constantly anticipating the instructional needs of the student and the classroom. Qualitative instruction, in which the teacher does not just assign more or less work but tailors the work to the student's unique instructional needs, is another characteristic of differentiated instruction. A third characteristic is formative assessment; that is, the teacher uses the assessments given in the classroom to modify instruction for the student. In differentiated instruction, the teacher takes multiple approaches to the content presented, instruction process, and student products, then tries to find the best match between the student and the instruction. Of course, differentiated instruction is also student centered and engages the student at a level appropriate for that student. Differentiated instruction differs from individualized instruction in that it mixes whole-class, small-group, and one-on-one instruction. This characteristic of differentiated instruction is important because it allows the teacher to effectively manage the classroom as four or five groups rather than as thirty individual students. Finally, differentiated instruction is flexible and evolving. In other words, the teacher begins with an instructional plan, then modifies the plan based on the student's progress.

While you may or may not be able to use differentiated instruction as the core instructional technique in your classroom, many of the characteristics can be used in individualized learning modules that can be delivered to one student or a few students on an as-needed basis.

THE INCLUSIVE CLASSROOM: AN OVERVIEW

One of the biggest challenges that the classroom teacher may face is the inclusive classroom. Historically, students with impairments, such as mental retardation and learning disabilities, received support services outside the regular education classroom. In fact, in the early days of special education, children were often completely isolated from the regular school to the point that they did not participate in any school activities. With the passage of PL94–142 the term "least restrictive environment" came into being. This meant that students were given services in such a way that they could participate as much as possible in the regular education classroom. This frequently meant that they were "pulled out" of the regular classroom for parts of the school day to receive services in another part of the school.

With inclusion, students receive all of their services in the regular education classroom. The Exceptional Children's teacher comes to the classroom to work with the students while the general curriculum is still being taught. When inclusion works well, the child receives a much more effective instructional program while benefiting from being with his or her peers during the regular school day. The implications for regular classroom teachers are significant because they must have a flexible classroom in which different students and multiple adults will be working at the same time on different things. It also means that regular classroom teachers must be able to work very closely with the Exceptional Children's teacher on a case-by-case basis so that the services being provided to the child are very tightly integrated in the child's entire educational program. Differentiated instruction can help general classroom teachers meet these challenges and at the same time provide a way to more fully integrate limited technological resources into the regular classroom.

As is the case with all teaching, much more work has to go on behind the scenes and prior to the actual instruction to make differentiated instruction work. For most students, this takes place with the IEP.

TECHNOLOGY AND THE INDIVIDUAL EDUCATION PLAN

An Individual Education Plan (IEP) is the blueprint for how the education of students with exceptionalities needs to be carried out. It is a key component of special education. Chapter 1 discussed the concept of an IEP at length.

What is important to note about an IEP is that included in this document are the requirements for the instructional program that the student will receive and the ways in which the student will be evaluated. This will include any assistive/adaptive technology that the student will need. The IEP will also specify any remedial technologies and how those technologies can be used in the regular classroom. The IEP should be the guiding document for the types of technologies used with the student in the classroom.

The classroom teacher should be involved at every stage of the formation of the IEP and can have a great deal to say about its contents. The classroom teacher is, after all, the one person who has the most instructional contact with the student and the best "sense" of how the student is performing academically. It is also important for the classroom teacher to be very involved in the IEP process if the student will be in an inclusive environment because the instructional strategies spelled out in the IEP will have an impact on the classroom environment. The formation of the IEP is also the time when the Exceptional Children's teacher and the classroom teacher begin to form a working partnership to help meet the needs of the student. This partnership needs to be encouraged through frequent consultations during the instructional process, not just when the IEP is being written. This allows for proactive planning and ensures that both the Exceptional Children's teacher and classroom teacher are working in parallel to best benefit the student.

Two issues that are important to pay attention to when the IEP is being written are the degree to which technology will be used for instruction and how technology will be used when the student is taking a standardized test. With regard to instruction, students with disabilities must receive appropriate assistive technologies. This may mean that students have their own laptop or may have specialized input devices such as keyboards and mice in the classroom. Students will be unique in terms of the technologies they will require and how they will use them. Assessment is another area where technology can play a big role in the student's academic success. Unfortunately, the degree to which technology can be used during assessment is, to a large extent, controlled by the policies of the state where the student resides. In addition to extended time, a student may be able to use word processing to take written tests, but spell check may have to be disabled. Students may be able to use calculators in some types of testing situations but not others. In these cases, the Exceptional Children's teacher will know the laws regarding testing modifications in the state where the IEP is being written. It is important that once these modifications are spelled out, the classroom teacher should follow these modifications when the student is receiving standardized assessments. Students should also receive instruction as to how these modifications will work for them so that they do not become confused when the assessment is given.

Technology and Differentiated Instruction: Mrs. Hargrave's Classroom

To see how differentiated instruction might work in a classroom situation, we will use the example of Mrs. Hargrave's classroom. Mrs. Hargrave has an inclusive classroom of elementary school students. In this unit, all of her students are reading a popular book. She has one group of students who have been identified as dyslexic. These students have no problem comprehending the subject matter but have difficulty decoding the text in the book. The second group consists of students in the regular education program. These students have average reading and comprehension abilities. The third group consists of academically gifted students who have already read the book at least three times.

Normally, Mrs. Hargrave has all of her students complete a traditional book report in which they describe the story of the book and draw their own conclusions about it.

Mrs. Hargrave decides to differentiate the assignment to better meet the needs of her students. She begins by assessing the students' technology competencies, asking them about their familiarity with programs such as word processing, Web surfing, and Web page creation. She finds that many of the students identified as academically gifted have at least some experience with Web page production, a fair amount of experience with word processing, and a great deal of experience with Web surfing. The students identified as dyslexic have a wide variety of technical skills from no skills with the computer to Web page development. The general education students also have a great deal of experience with computers, but their experiences have really focused on Web surfing and some word processing.

After this informal assessment, Mrs. Hargrave decides to differentiate her instruction at two levels. She begins by having all of the students read the book but in different ways. The students who have been identified as dyslexic listen to an audiotape of the book that Mrs. Hargrave has obtained from the Library for the Blind. These students listen in pairs or small groups with multiple headphones plugged into the tape player, using equipment provided by the Library for the Blind. If one student does not understand the text or gets lost, an assigned group leader stops and reviews the tape on the recorder.

The regular education students are grouped together and read the book to each other in pairs or small groups of three to four students. They are grouped based on their individual reading abilities so that stronger readers are paired or grouped with weaker readers. The students identified as academically gifted are asked to read the book independently with the understanding that they may ask the teacher for help at any time.

Once all of the students have finished the book, they work in pairs or small groups to write a traditional book report. The groups present their book reports to the class once they are completed. After the presentations, Mrs. Hargrave guides the class through an activity in which the best parts of each book report are collected and organized to make a "super" book report.

Mrs. Hargrave then reorders students by level of technology skill. Students with high technology skills are challenged to learn new Web authoring software that Mrs. Hargrave has just obtained from the district office. These students work together on a computer in the classroom to learn the technology tool.

Meanwhile, students with weak technology skills are asked to begin storyboarding the class project. A storyboard is a document that contains the full text for the interactive book report, descriptions of pictures for the report, and a graphical representation of how the content for the Web site will be organized.

The students with moderate technology skills are asked to type the book report so that it is digitally captured in the computer. They are also responsible for gathering multimedia elements such as pictures and links to areas of interest on the Web.

Once the storyboard is completed, Mrs. Hargrave then pairs each of the students with strong technology skills with groups of students with moderate to weak technology skills. The storyboard is also divided up so that each group has its own part of the storyboard. The students with advanced technology skills then help the students with weak technology skills create their own part of the class Web site. Since the Web site can be run from the computer's hard drive, each of the groups takes turns working on the classroom computer. Once the entire project is completed, each group presents its part of the entire class's Web site.

CULTURAL SENSITIVITY, GENDER EQUITY, AND THE USE OF TECHNOLOGY IN THE CLASSROOM

As technology is increasingly being used in the classroom to address the needs of diverse learners, many issues are being discovered that teachers should be aware of. One issue that has generated and continues to generate a significant amount of emphasis within education and the press is the use or, more appropriately, the lack of use of technology by minorities, students from low-socioeconomic backgrounds, and females. Awareness of this will help teachers become sensitive to what needs to take place for these students to benefit from the use of technology integrated into classroom instruction.

Cultural Sensitivity and the Digital Divide

The term "digital divide" indicates the gap that exists between those who have access to technology and those who do not. Despite the increased availability and use of technology in the classroom, the digital divide still exists. This divide contributes to bringing about a serious disconnect between those who have access to and training in the use of technology and those who do not (Hoffman & Novak, 1998; Pearson, 2001).

Minorities suffer most frequently from the effects of the digital divide (Bolt & Crawford, 2000). Minorities have historically not been exposed to technology in significant ways, often because technology has been viewed as being controlling rather than empowering. This perception is changing as minorities embrace the benefits that technology can provide.

Teachers need to make a conscious effort to help ensure that minorities have access to technology. Opportunities need to be deliberately created and provided that allow minorities as much time as possible to use technology in the classroom. Teachers should also model the use of technology to show that having skill in using technology can be empowering. By doing this, teachers can break down many of the fears that minorities and females have about technology so that technology is no longer perceived as a threat and instead becomes an empowering tool. One way in which this can occur is by differentiating instruction so that students are allowed to explore topics that are relevant to their situation.

An example of the process of differentiated instruction is a social studies unit in which students are learning about the Lewis and Clark expedition. Students view the Ken Burns documentary on the subject and then work in groups to research one of the historical figures of the expedition included on the companion PBS Web site. In addition to Sacagawea, another member of a minority who came along on the expedition was York, William Clark's slave. After some preliminary research, the student groups begin a Web log or Blog, a fictional journal written by each of these figures. Blogs are electronic journals available for viewing by others on the Internet. In these journals, students describe certain events of the expedition from their person's unique perspective. As the unit progresses, the teacher assigns groups to read each other's Blogs to see how the expedition is going from the perspective of another expedition member. In the middle of the unit, groups then switch Blogs and roles in the expedition to learn about the unique perspective of yet another expedition member.

USING TECHNOLOGY WITH ELL STUDENTS

ELL students, those whose primary language is not English (see Chapter 2), are typically part of a minority. These students often have difficulties mastering English, which creates several barriers for them in mastering content. Along with challenges to literacy in English, students may well be illiterate in their primary language. This compounds the challenges faced by the classroom teacher because not only do these students lack English skills, they may also lack the basic skills needed to read at all. The ELL student may also have a learning disability that can interfere with learning these basic skills. At the other extreme is the ELL student who is actually gifted. These students pose unique challenges for the classroom teacher who must not only help them acquire English but must also challenge them in their native language. A good starting point for the teacher is to have a very good grasp of where each student is in terms of skill development. Once this is understood, the teacher can then group ELL students appropriately so as to meet their unique needs.

Technology can provide teachers with some very useful tools that can help them address these needs. In Chapter 3, we talked about Web sites that can translate English into Spanish as well as the reverse. You can have ELL students who are academically advanced do a mini research project that involves accessing English-only Web sites to find out about some topic. If they have problems interpreting the English-only site, they can generate a translation of the English-only site through the interpretative site. Once they have completed the paper in English, you can then have them run the paper through software that will interpret the text back into Spanish to see if the text being read is what they had intended to write in the first place.

English language difficulties can also exacerbate the often-difficult endeavor of fitting into the classroom culture. ELL students may experience isolation and frustration from being unable to communicate effectively with the teacher and classmates. This can lead to classroom management and discipline problems. In order to address these issues, you should look for occasions to provide ELL students with positive opportunities so that they can feel they are a part of the classroom culture without denying their own culture.

Because ELL students tend to have much less access to technology than do their peers (Neuman, 1994), the teacher needs to carefully plan for the inclusion of ELL students in classroom instruction that involves technology. A hallmark of this planning is the instructional environment that is created for the ELL student. Technology use for ELL students needs to be part of a learning environment that encourages discovery learning and connections to larger communities (including their own native community) (Ovando & Collier, 1998). Another instructional principle for ELL students is the creation of an active and engaging environment (Liaw, 1997). "Children need to be able to interact with each other so that learning through communication can occur. Computers can facilitate this type of environment. By using electronic tools such as email, moos, and video conferencing the computer can act as a tool to increase verbal exchange" (Ybarra & Green, 2003).

Typical use of technology by ELL students tends to be through "drill and practice" software in which students interact with English in an isolated manner. Although "drill and practice" software has its place, it should not be the only way in which ELL students interact with technology. With the wide variety of technology tools that are available, teachers have many options for creating meaningful instruction for the ELL student. A few principles can help the classroom teacher when using technology to facilitate ELL instruction (Brown, 1993; Butler-Pascoe & Wiburg, 2003).

Effective ELL Instruction Uses Technologies That Will Let Students Create Their Own Work

This can be as simple as having students create word-processed documents that incorporate digital pictures into video, and audiotapes that illustrate the student's cultural heritage. The most involved examples include the creation of multimedia Web sites that combine digitized video, audio, and pictures with text and links to create a rich exploration of a particular culture or language.

Whenever Possible, Allow Students to Capture Oral Records of Their Work

ELL students can use very inexpensive tape recorders bought at a local office supply store. The vast majority of computers in classrooms today have audio capture cards that, along with an inexpensive microphone, can also capture examples of ELL students' work that can be embedded in *PowerPoint* presentations or small Web sites.

Have Students Work Together in Pairs or Small Groups to Write Collaboratively

These groups can be a mix of ELL and non-ELL students. By grouping students together, teachers can help ELL students improve their English language skills through immersion and reinforcement. If a writing assignment involves some aspect of ELL students' culture, then they can also become "experts" on a topic and so improve their sense of self-worth.

Have ELL Students Use Technology to Create Electronic Book Reports

Rather than just having ELL students create a written book report, have them audiotape their book report in both their native language and English. If a video camera is available, a videotaped book report can be created. Students can then go back to either the audiotape or videotape to review the report not only for content but also for their mastery of English.

Use Technology to Help ELL
Students Engage in Critical Reflection

Once students have captured a book report on audiotape, they can play the tape not only for their mastery of English but also for a review of their thoughts and ideas. A common activity in collaborative writing exercises is to have students review each other's work not only for mechanics but also for content. Once students have reviewed each other's work, they give feedback that the first student can then use for revisions.

Use Technology to Facilitate Communication
With Students From Other Places in the World

This is perhaps one of the most powerful uses of the Internet. By establishing connections with classrooms from around the world, students can communicate with students who not only speak their own native language but who also can reinforce cultural ties. At the same time, students in the class who are native English speakers can get to know the ELL student's cultural experience a little better and so have a greater appreciation for the ELL student. This can be done with e-mail pals from other classrooms. Many Web sites provide international directories of school Web sites that teachers can use to contact other teachers who are also interested in establishing international e-mail pals.

GENDER EQUITY AND THE USE OF TECHNOLOGY

The classroom teacher should also be aware that inequities exist in how often and in what ways females use technology in comparison to males (Gilley, 2002). Boys typically use computers as toys, while girls use computers to accomplish specific tasks. Boys often tend to become "obsessed" with using technology, while girls tend to be more occasional users. This has led to boys being encouraged by adults to use technology (Margolis & Fisher, 2001). In spite of this, research indicates that girls are just as capable as boys in effectively using technology even though female perceptions indicate that they believe they have less experience and knowledge than males in using technology (Gilley, 2002; Mathis, 2002). In order to address the unique needs of girls with respect to technology, teachers need to ensure that girls have equal access to technology and encourage them to use it in a variety of meaningful ways.

How can teachers encourage girls to use technology? Creating deliberate opportunities for girls to use technology in a variety of ways will go a long way to addressing the gender gap in technology. Also, teachers, especially female teachers, can be role models for girls by using technology in the classroom.

The teacher can also use the following techniques when addressing the issue of gender with respect to technology in the classroom.

Class Management Strategies That May Help Give Girls Equal Access to Computing Tools

• Mr. Wayne's classroom has five computers that he uses for small-group activities. However, the boys in the classroom always seem to wind up actually sitting in front of the keyboard, while the girls in the group always seem to be talking to one another. To solve this problem, Mr. Wayne established a rotation schedule so that no individual student dominated the keyboard and mouse. Requiring every student to put in time as the keyboard/mouse operator may help to give girls equal access to computing tools.

• Ms. Martin used her computer lab time to introduce new concepts such as scanning to the entire class. After her presentations, however, the few scanners available to the class tended to be dominated by the boys. To fix this problem, she decided to do small-group instruction in which she would make sure that everyone in the group had an equal opportunity to learn how to use the equipment and allow the girls in the class to build confidence when using the equipment.

• Mrs. Richards finds that she is conveying the technology skills to the girls in her high school classroom but is having a hard time getting them excited about using technology. During career day, she invites Ms. Neil, a local graphic designer, to come and talk to the class about how she uses computers in her day-to-day work.

USING TECHNOLOGY IN THE CONTENT AREAS TO FACILITATE INSTRUCTION WITH DIVERSE LEARNERS

The goal of this section is to provide several examples of how technology can be used within content areas to help meet the needs of diverse learners who are part of all classrooms. Many of the example activities provided can be used in various content areas. It is important to note that the examples are only a representative sample of the almost endless possibilities that exist. Our hope is that the examples will provide a starting point for you to begin experimenting with integrating technology into the curriculum to meet the needs of your diverse learners. We hope that you take these ideas and build on them to construct your own unique ideas that more closely fit the needs of your students.

Art

Art is very well suited for the integration of technology. Most relatively new computers are well equipped with the capabilities to allow students to develop their creativity through the creation of digital artwork. There are numerous graphic software programs (see Table 4.1) available that students can use to create and edit their own artwork. The artwork can be distributed in many different ways—printed, distributed on a CD-ROM or DVD, or simply viewed on a computer or television screen.

Students with physical disabilities may have difficulties manipulating a standard computer mouse. As mentioned in Chapter 3, numerous alternative devices can be used instead of a standard computer mouse—trackball, touch screen, and graphic tablet. These devices make it easier for students with disabilities to use the computer to develop their own digital artwork.

Table 4.1   Graphic Development Software Programs

Professional Quality	Kid-Friendly
Adobe Photoshop Adobe Illustrator Macromedia Freehand	IntelliTools KidPix Microsoft Paint

A variety of art activities can help students with diverse needs meet a wide range of learning outcomes. Described below are several of these activities.

Activity A: Comprehension—Recalling Facts or Understanding Main Ideas

Mrs. Snow's junior high school class is reading *Fahrenheit 451*. At the same time, Mr. Reardon is covering a popular graphics program in the computer lab. Both teachers decided to team-teach a lesson in which students can use a graphics program to draw images that illustrate the facts or main idea(s) from the book. This activity is great for the students in Mrs. Snow's class who have difficulties with written language because they can demonstrate their comprehension through images rather than words.

Activity B: Higher-Order Thinking
Skills—Sequencing Events or Making Predictions

Ms. Lee's students are learning about the life cycle of the butterfly. Normally, she has students learn about the order of the stages by putting a series of cards in order. This year she decides to have students import pictures of the life cycle into a *PowerPoint* presentation. As a part of the presentation, students have to put the slides of the stages in the correct order and include descriptions of the processes that are occurring at each stage of the butterfly's development.

Activity C: Expressing Emotions and Feelings

Mrs. Ferguson is an art teacher at a junior high school who wants to use technology in her classroom. She has several ELL students who have expressed an interest in art from their home cultures. Mr. Miller is a computer teacher in the same school and is interested in creating a unit that introduces the concept of digital photography. Together they devise a lesson in which students create a virtual museum. Some students create a variety of original artwork from sculptures to drawings. Students then digitize these works in a variety of ways including digital photographs and QuickTime VR movies that render three-dimensional representations of objects such as sculptures. Students then create a virtual museum in which they display their work and provide a narrative that explains the inspiration for their creation and how they felt while they were creating the work.

Activity D: Fine-Motor Skill Development

Ms. Garza, the art teacher in an elementary school, has several students in her class who have problems with fine-motor coordination. In order to address the unique learning needs of these students, she develops a lesson in which students use writing tablets and a graphic program to create an original drawing. So that they can better work with the tablets, she increases the screen revolution on the computers to make all of the objects appear two to three times larger than they normally would. This allows students more "wiggle room" for drawing objects. She also shows students how to use the "snap to grid" feature in the drawing program so that they can easily create squares, circles, and other objects with regular edges. By using a drawing program, students are also more easily able to correct mistakes with the undo feature in the program.

Activity E: Nonverbal Communication

Mr. Massy, a teacher in an elementary school, has several students who have been identified as learning disabled and have difficulty with writing assignments. Rather than have these students write a traditional story, he decides to have them use graphics or paint software to express concepts as well as feelings by creating an animated story with *KidPix*. Students have to create an outline of their story. This outline then becomes the guide that they use to develop the animation.

Figure 4.1   The National Arts and Disability Center at UCLA

This organization provides a variety of excellent art activities for individuals with disabilities. It offers numerous links to Web sites and other resources that teachers can use as they integrate technology with art to assist students with disabilities.

SOURCE: http://nadc.ucla.edu/.

Language Arts

Technology integration into language arts can be extremely beneficial for students with diverse needs. Technology allows students to work on essential reading and writing skills and to express themselves in ways beyond writing. Below are a few examples of how language arts activities can be adopted for diverse learners by using technology.

Activity A: WordWebs–Prewriting

Mrs. Kremer is teaching prewriting to her middle school students. She decides to have her students use *Kidspiration* to organize their thoughts. While this software is helpful for all of the students in her classroom, she is particularly interested in using it because of her students who have difficulties with written language. *Kidspiration* allows her students to create word webs with images to organize their thoughts as they brainstorm. After her students have created their word webs, they print out their work to help them when they are writing. Mrs. Kremer also has her students convert their word webs into outlines that they can then import directly into many popular word-processing programs to get the students started in their writing assignments.

Activity B: Word Processing

Mrs. Yamada has several students in her elementary school classroom who have been identified as having writing difficulties. She knows that word-processing software can be a valuable tool for students with writing difficulties and decides to use Riverdeep's *Storybook Weaver Deluxe* to help her students with their writing. After engaging in a prewriting exercise in which the students create an outline for their assignments, Mrs. Yamada has her students use their outlines to write a completed paper. While her students are working on their paper, she shows them how to use features common to word processors such as cutting, pasting, spell checking, and grammar checking. By having her students edit their documents, she can break the writing process down into manageable steps so students do not have to deal with creating text, the mechanics of writing, and formatting all at the same time. She also makes her students aware of some of the limitations of word processing such as the fact that the software will not flag words that are spelled correctly but will flag words that are incorrectly used in the document. She also shows students how to save and print their documents.

Some of Mrs. Yamada's students also have difficulty typing. To help these students, Mrs. Yamada has them use voice recognition. This type of program allows students to speak into a microphone so that the text is entered directly into word-processing software. Students can then use the other features of the word-processing software to edit their documents.

Activity C: Audio and Video Recordings

Ms. Sivan's middle school class has students with a wide range of abilities. In addition to students with writing disabilities, Ms. Sivan has several students who have been classified as academically gifted. To help all of her students learn about writing, she decides to have them work in teams to create brief movies that they can then later turn into written assignments. This will give the gifted students a chance to engage in an enrichment activity while helping the other students gain a better perspective on the writing process.

Ms. Sivan begins by having all of the groups create a storyboard of their story, which is much like creating a story outline. She then has some of the students do the narration for their videos on the computer using a simple microphone (*Sound Recorder*, which comes with all Windows operating systems, can be used for this). While some students do this narration, other students videotape the action that they want to use for their projects. Then, using a video-editing program (such as *iMovie* available on the Macintosh or *Movie Maker* available for the PC), students bring the narration and video segments together into a story.

Activity D: Digital Books

Mr. Spinks's elementary school classroom has several ELL learners. In order to facilitate a writing assignment, he decides to use a program called *MeBooks* to create an E-book. The software allows students to focus the content of their book on themselves by guiding them through a prewriting exercise to develop the content for their books. He begins his unit by introducing the students to the program. He then has them use *MeBooks* to create a written document. The software provides students with an opportunity to share their culture as well as themselves. He also has his students include pictures of family members, pets, or friends (which can be scanned, drawn, or digitally photographed—depending on the technology available) in their digital books. Additionally, he has his students include an audio of their own voice. This gives ELL students the opportunity to include audio of their native language, allowing them to feel good about their culture by being able to share it with others (Green & Peerless, 2001). The assignment concludes with a book report that students give at the end of the unit.

Activity E: Word Recognition–Reading Practice

Mrs. Agre has several students in her elementary classroom who have been identified with dyslexia. These students, who have difficulties reading, can benefit from a variety of different software designed to act as tutorials as well as digital books, which can help read the book back to the child. Mrs. Agre decides to use several books from Broderbund's *Living Books* series. In addition to presenting students with the text of the book, the series can also read the text back to the student, and the students can have the program reread the text back to them simply by pointing and clicking with the computer's mouse. This can help students practice word recognition and other repetitive tasks. This can help Mrs. Agre since it allows her to work with other students. Once her students have finished with their books, she follows up the activity by asking them a series of questions to check for comprehension.

Mathematics

Technology can be exceptionally useful in helping students work on a variety of math skills from basic operations (e.g., addition and subtraction) to more complex math skills (e.g., logical thinking needed to solve geometric proofs or algebraic equations). Computing tools are especially useful in math because of the power that computers have in quickly processing numbers. This means that students are free to explore more complex mathematical concepts as well as "what if" scenarios more quickly than if they had to work out problems with paper and pencil. Below are several scenarios that illustrate how technology can be integrated into math instruction.

Activity A: Calculators

Mr. Sharkey is teaching his students the Pythagorean theorem. He has several students who have been identified as learning disabled. They have difficulties with basic math calculations such as multiplication, but interestingly enough, they enjoy more complex problems such as solving proofs in geometry. In order to facilitate his students' mastery of this mathematical concept, he has them use calculators to do the more basic operations of multiplication and division. This allows them to go through the process of solving math problems without getting stuck on the calculations. Mr. Sharkey is careful to show students each of the steps of the Pythagorean theorem so that they master them. To reinforce this, he initially has students make the calculations with handheld calculators and then has them make the same calculations using *Excel* spreadsheets. By having his students set up the formula in the spreadsheet, he has been able to reinforce the concepts in multiple ways.

Activity B: Digital Manipulatives

Ms. Bourlier has been using manipulatives to help her students with mental retardation master basic math skills such as addition, subtraction, multiplication, and division. She knows that manipulatives allow her students to tactilely work through math problems and at the same time visually see what is being done.

This year she has been moved from a rather large room in which her students had plenty of space to do manipulatives to a rather small room, which does not provide her with much space at all. In order to address this space problem, she decides to use *IntelliTools Math* to provide her students with digital manipulatives to practice a variety of math problems, especially addition and subtraction. She is able to take her students down to the computer lab where they can work on these activities. Since the computer lab also has Internet access, she supplements the activities in *IntelliTools Math* with activities from http://matti.usu.edu/nlvm/nav/vlibrary.html. This Web site, which was funded by a National Science Foundation grant, offers Web-based manipulatives in numerous math areas.

Activity C: Programming Languages–Logical Thinking

Mr. Boggs teaches math at the junior high school level and has several students who have been identified as academically gifted. They are frequently bored with content that other students in his class are struggling to master. In order to provide activities that can best meet the needs of these students, Mr. Boggs uses *MicroWorlds Logo* (http://www.microworlds.com/), a programming language that allows students to use both their creativity and logical thinking as they develop different multimedia projects. The students are able to use this basic programming language to develop their own programs. While developing these programs, they are reinforcing the mathematical concepts that they are quickly mastering in the classroom.

Activity D: Expressive Math

Ms. Birtolo has one student in her high school math class who consistently has problems arriving at correct answers or has difficulty with numbers (dyscalculia—see Chapter 2), but is able to describe how she has arrived at a particular answer. To better assess this student's ability to solve math problems, Ms. Birtolo has the student use a tape recorder to explain how the student would work (or has worked out) her math problems. Ms. Birtolo can gain many insights by listening to how her student has attempted to process through the math problems. She can also use these audiotapes to detect problems and prescribe remediation.

Activity E: Spreadsheets

Mr. Hidalgo teaches introductory statistics and has several students who have an easier time grasping mathematical concepts if they can see information represented in a graphical format. To address the needs of these students, Mr. Hidalgo sets up an assignment in which these students have to use spreadsheet software (a variety of spreadsheet applications are available from Microsoft, Apple, and others) to store, manipulate, and perform statistical calculations. After students have solved a series of statistical problems, he has them create pictorial representations of the data by using the same software to create a variety of graphs and charts.

Science

For years computers have played an important role in scientific exploration. Computers are able to re-create complex models of physical and organic systems. In the classroom, computers can meet the needs of a wide variety of students, from those who need remediation on certain scientific concepts to those who need enhanced instruction. Recent developments in three-dimensional modeling can even allow students new perspectives through the graphical representation of anything from an atom to a galaxy. Below are four examples from the wide range showing how computers can be used in science-oriented instructional situations.

Activity A: Data Gathering and Manipulation

Mrs. Prentaz is teaching a science unit on weather. She has a variety of students ranging from those who are gifted to a couple of students who have difficulty with mathematics. She recently received a small classroom grant that she used to purchase two inexpensive GPS units. GPS stands for global positioning system and can be used to accurately pinpoint a location on the earth's surface down to a few feet. GPS is used for a wide variety of applications. To differentiate the instruction in this unit, she has the entire class collect a variety of weather data and record these data into a spreadsheet. She has her students use the GPS units to record their exact position. While the students are collecting their data, she also has them use the GPS to precisely record where they have recorded their data. She then has them compare their readings with weather data collected from the Internet. Then, based on the data they have collected, Mrs. Prentaz has students make weather predictions that they compare with the predictions made on the Internet and actual weather events. Students who are having difficulties with calculations can benefit from the spreadsheet's ability to do quick mathematical calculations. Students who are academically gifted have the experience of working with an actual GPS unit and learning more about how these systems work.

Activity B: Robotics: Lego MindStorms

Lego MindStorms is a robotic development system that provides students with opportunities to create their own robots (and other devices). Mr. Parker teaches in an elementary school and is interested in developing a unit that would combine math and science in such a way as to be able to meet the needs of several students in his classroom who have been identified as learning disabled. These students tend to do better if they can engage in activities that require them to work with projects. Mr. Parker finds that *Lego MindStorms* (http://mindstorms.lego.com/eng/default.asp) meets these needs. Using a small grant that he recently received, he purchases a *Lego MindStorms* set. *Lego MindStorms* uses regular Lego building blocks along with specialized motors and sensors that allow a student to build a variety of robots. Mr. Parker developed a series of science units in which students have to build several projects that allow them to explore a variety of science concepts, such as motion, levers, and pulleys.

Activity C: Ask an Expert

Ms. Davis's high school science classroom is engaged in several projects exploring a variety of different concepts. She has differentiated the instruction in their room to better meet the needs of her students who have a variety of learning styles and abilities. Some of the students have reached a point in their work where they are unable to find information about their subject. Ms. Davis has a direct connection to the Internet in her classroom. With this connection, her students can log on to the Web and find sites where they can ask questions of scientists (one such site is http://www .askanexpert.com/). With this information her students are able to complete their assignment. Prior to their accessing the Internet, she has them do a type of prewriting exercise in which they refine the questions that they need to ask so as not to overwhelm their expert with frivolous questions. Before submitting questions, Ms. Davis also has students hypothesize what they believe will be the expert's response. Once the response is provided, student responses are compared and contrasted.

Activity D: Time-Lapse Photography

Digital cameras produce immediate results (no need to wait for film to be developed), making them ideal for time-lapse photography activities. These types of activities are well suited for students who have difficulty with higher-order concepts that involve change over a period of time. Ms. Betz has her students engage in just such an activity by having them take repeated snapshots of the sky. Her students take a picture of the sky every ten minutes so that things such as the movement of clouds and the sun's path are revealed to the students. Ms. Betz has her students import these images into Apple's *iMovie* to produce a presentation that reveals a previously undetectable pattern.

Social Studies

A major goal of social studies education is to teach students to under- stand what it means to live in a democratic society. There are numerous elements to this process, some of which are learning to be a productive citizen and respecting other people and their cultures (as well as under- standing one's own culture). Technology can be a wonderful source, espe- cially the Internet, in helping students connect to and learn from others, which can be beneficial in helping reach the major goals of social studies education. The goals of the social studies curriculum provide excellent opportunities for including ELL students such as connecting with students from across the country and around the world. Social studies activities also provide many opportunities for the use and creation of rich multimedia documents that can illustrate many concepts in new and exciting ways.

Activity A: Key-Pals

Understanding other cultures is a key element of social studies. Typically, the more one knows about others, the less likely prejudices and stereotypes will be perpetuated. Additionally, ELL students benefit not only from exposure to their own native culture but also from exposure to other cultures. In her middle school classroom, Mrs. Ray uses key-pals so that students can use the Internet (specifically, e-mail) to connect to other students around the United States and the world to exchange electronic letters (e-mail messages). Many key-pals sites are available on the Internet and can be found using a simple Google search. To provide her students with e-mail addresses, Mrs. Ray sets up a series of free e-mail addresses using Gaggle.net (http://www.gaggle.net/). The links that Mrs. Ray found led her to e-mail lists of other teachers who have expressed a willingness to let their students e-mail other students. After she has identified appropriate teachers willing to participate in her unit, she gets information about the students that will help her students form appropriate questions for their key-pals. She then has her students compose e-mail messages that not only pose these questions but also introduce themselves to their key-pals. Any of her ELL students who are fluent in the key-pals' native language take the lead in composing the initial messages to help interpret these messages. Once the initial messages are sent out and the replies come back, Mrs. Ray has her students report on the replies and then draft their replies. Mrs. Ray makes sure that the questions being asked of the key-pals are congruent with the curriculum. This process continues until the end of the current social studies unit. If Mrs. Ray determines that the next social studies unit is appropriate, she has her students ask their key-pals another round of questions. Of course, Mrs. Ray also provides time for her students to answer questions posed by her students' key-pals.

Activity B: Virtual Expeditions

Most students will never be able to travel to different locations around the world. Virtual expeditions are real-life travels, typically consisting of a team of individuals who explore different locations around the world. Mr. Pan's classroom is studying cultures from around the world and he would like to supplement the textbook readings his students are doing with nontext information. This is for the benefit of both those students who are having difficulties with reading and those students who need to supplement the information available to them in the class text. He locates a virtual expedition online, which is available for free to public school students. This is a bit unusual as most online expeditions do require a fee. He begins the activity by dividing his class into teams. Each team digitally documents its travels by posting information (e.g., text, video, audio, and images) about what is taking place to the Web. During this activity, his students access a Web site where the information is posted and where they can follow the progress of the expedition. This gives Mr. Pan's students the sense that they are actually traveling with the expedition. Once the expeditions have concluded, Mr. Pan has his students incorporate the photographs and text from the expedition into a report that is then presented to the class.

Activity C: Primary Source Documents

Mrs. Chao has several students who have been identified as academically gifted in her classroom. These students constantly need supplemental activities to keep them engaged in the curriculum. For this grading period, Mrs. Chao decides to have these students access primary source documents, which are important artifacts that aid in the understanding of history. With digital storage capabilities getting better and less expensive, many primary source documents are being made available digitally on the World Wide Web and on CD-ROM or DVD. Mrs. Chao finds that her students have few problems accessing documents about U.S. history. Before she begins this unit, she makes sure that all of her students have read and understand the school's Acceptable Use Policy (an AUP describes the acceptable and unacceptable uses of the Internet that can take place at school) and has her students' parents sign a copy of the AUP before the students begin this unit. She has her students use search engines such as *Yahooligans* (http://www.yahooligans.com/) as their primary search engines. Such engines are designed so as to minimize the possibility that students will accidentally access an inappropriate site. Of course, Mrs. Chao knows that no technology is completely foolproof and so monitors the progress of her students closely.

Mrs. Chao's students easily find artifacts such as the Declaration of Independence online at a variety of U.S. government Web sites. She also locates several CD-ROMs that contain audio and video clips that students can use to research the implications of the Declaration of Independence. One of these is Martin Luther King's "I have a dream speech," which puts a very real face on some of the abstract ideas being studied in her class. At the end of the unit, Mrs. Chao has her students write an audio and video report that incorporates media from a wide variety of these documents. These digitized reports provide her students with several alternative methods for expressing their thoughts and ideas. She gives her students several options to record their audio and video on regular analog devices (audiocassettes or VCR tapes) or using digital means such as a computer.

Of course, many of her students choose to use the computer to create their reports. Once her students are done with their reports, they share them using the World Wide Web. They also save their Web sites by burning them onto CD-ROMs that can then be sent home and/or archived.

SUMMARY

A common saying goes something like this, "If the only tool you have in your tool belt is a hammer, then pretty soon all of your problems begin to look like nails."

As we have explored the uses of technology with students from a wide variety of backgrounds and with widely ranging abilities, we hope that we have given you a few more tools in your instructional tool belt. The integration of a variety of technologies into the classroom can provide learners with unique opportunities to help meet their diverse needs. Technology can be an empowering tool. For it to be empowering, however, teachers must be deliberate and thoughtful in how it is integrated and utilized in the classroom. This is not only true for students with a variety of impairments but is also true for ELL and gifted and talented students. Issues of gender and technology have also become issues as computing becomes more pervasive in our society and schools. But while technology can be used as a tool to solve these problems, it is ultimately the teacher who wields all of the tools that can enrich and empower students.

FOR FURTHER APPLICATION

A wealth of information and resources exists that supports teachers' professional development in terms of integrating technology into the diverse classroom. A Google search can help you locate many of these. When searching, be sure that the Web site you find is associated with a well-known entity such as the federal government or a professional organization like the Council for Exceptional Children. In this section, we include Web sites affiliated with well-known entities that can lead you to many additional resources. Along with these resources, we also include Web sites that take you directly to lesson plans and other materials that can help you better integrate technology into the diverse classroom.

Professional Resources Web Sites

- The Council for Exceptional Children (http://www.cec.sped.org/)
- The American Association of People with Disabilities (http://www.aapd-dc.org/)

- The American Association on Mental Retardation (http://www.aamr.org/)
- ERIC Clearinghouse on Language and Linguistics (http://www.cal.org/ericcll/digest/)
- U.S. Department of Education (http://www.ed.gov/index.html)

Lesson Plans and Other Resources

- Thirteen Ed Online (http://www.thirteen.org/edonline/lessons/)
- ERIC Resources for Teachers (http://www.ericsp.org/pages/resources/lessonplans.html)
- Diversity Learning (resources for Canadian and American teachers) (http://www.diversitylearning.ca/index.asp)
- Learn NC (http://www.learnnc.org/)
- PBS Teacher Source (http://www.pbs.org/teachersource/)

Appendix A

Diverse Learners and Technologies

To help you more easily find a specific technology discussed in this book, we have created this table. If you are unsure about which technologies are most appropriate for a specific category of diverse learner, you can scan the table and then use the index to find the specific page where the technology is discussed. The check mark in each box indicates an appropriate technology for the area of diversity listed at the top of the column.

Technology	English Language Learners	Physical Disabilities	Cognitive Disabilities	Learning Disabilities	Gifted and Talented
AlphaSmart				✓	
Alternative Keyboards		✓			
Amplification Devices		✓			
Arthur's Teacher Trouble	✓		✓	✓	
Babelfish	✓		✓	✓	
BigKeys Keyboard		✓			
Blabbermouth	✓		✓		
Calculators		✓	✓	✓	✓
CCTV Monitor			✓	✓	
Chat (IM or ICQ)	✓			✓	✓
Closed Captioning		✓			
Computer Tablet		✓		✓	
"Drill and Skill" Software	✓		✓	✓	
E-mail	✓			✓	✓
Eye Movement Activation Switch		✓			
FM Listening System		✓			
Free Translation	✓				

Technology	English Language Learners	Physical Disabilities	Cognitive Disabilities	Learning Disabilities	Gifted and Talented
Hands-Free Control		✓			
Hearing-Aid-Compatible Phones		✓			
Hearing Aids		✓			
HyperStudio					✓
IBM ViaVoice		✓	✓	✓	
IntelliKeys		✓	✓	✓	
IntelliPics			✓	✓	
IntelliTools (Math)			✓	✓	
Internet Video/Audio	✓	✓	✓	✓	✓
iVisit	✓	✓	✓	✓	✓
JAWS		✓	✓	✓	
Key Repeat Rate Control		✓	✓	✓	
Keyboard Macros		✓	✓	✓	
Language Translation Software	✓				
Large Computer Monitor		✓	✓	✓	
Lego MindStorms				✓	✓
Life Skills Software			✓	✓	

Technology	English Language Learners	Physical Disabilities	Cognitive Disabilities	Learning Disabilities	Gifted and Talented
MicroWorlds Logo				✓	✓
MOOs and MUDs	✓				✓
NetMeeting	✓				✓
Optical Character Recognition (OCR)		✓	✓	✓	
Phone Headset		✓			
PowerPoint				✓	✓
Programming Language				✓	✓
Reader Rabbit			✓	✓	
Receiver Holder		✓			
Riverdeep			✓	✓	
Robotic Devices				✓	✓
SCATIR Switch		✓			
Screen Magnification Software		✓	✓	✓	
Screen Readers	✓	✓	✓	✓	
Sequential Keystroke Input Software		✓	✓	✓	
Speaker Phone		✓			

Technology	English Language Learners	Physical Disabilities	Cognitive Disabilities	Learning Disabilities	Gifted and Talented
Speech Recognition		✓	✓	✓	
Speech Synthesizers	✓	✓	✓	✓	
Speech-to-Text Software	✓	✓	✓	✓	
Speed Dialing		✓			
Spreadsheet Software				✓	✓
StageCast Creator				✓	✓
Tactile Output		✓			
Telephony		✓			
Teletypewriter (TTY)		✓			
Text-to-Speech Software	✓	✓	✓	✓	
Touch Screen		✓			
Trackball		✓			
Translation Software	✓				
Volume Control		✓	✓		
Web Authoring Software	✓		✓	✓	✓
WebQuest	✓		✓	✓	✓
Word Prediction Software		✓	✓	✓	
Word Processing	✓	✓	✓	✓	✓

Appendix B

Diverse Learners and Instructional Strategies

To help you better match a student with a specific type of technology and instructional strategy, we have created the following table. In this table you will find the categories we discussed in Chapter 2, along with the instructional strategies and technologies we discussed in Chapter 4. The check marks in each box indicate which strategy and technology is appropriate for each type of student.

Instructional Strategy	Technology	English Language Learners	Physical Disabilities	Cognitive Disabilities	Learning Disabilities	Gifted and Talented
Ask an Expert	E-mail	✓			✓	✓
Audio-Based Book Report	Tape Recorder	✓	✓	✓	✓	✓
Building a Robot	Lego MindStorms				✓	✓
Collaborative Research	Word Processing World Wide Web Online Resources	✓	✓	✓	✓	✓
Collaborative Writing	Word Processing	✓	✓	✓	✓	✓
Computer Art	Graphics Program		✓		✓	✓
Creating a Virtual Museum	QuickTime VR Web Authoring Software	✓			✓	✓
Creating an Animated Story	KidPix			✓	✓	✓
Digital Manipulatives	IntelliTools Math		✓	✓	✓	
Discovery Learning	Online Resources	✓	✓	✓	✓	✓
Drill and Practice Activities	Riverdeep			✓	✓	
Electronic Book Report	Web Authoring Software	✓	✓	✓	✓	✓
Electronic Journals	Web Log	✓	✓	✓	✓	✓

Instructional Strategy	Technology	English Language Learners	Physical Disabilities	Cognitive Disabilities	Learning Disabilities	Gifted and Talented
English/Native Language Research Project	Audio Recorder Online Resources	✓				
Expressive Math	Audiotape				✓	
Key-Pals	Web Directory E-mail	✓			✓	✓
Lewis and Clark Multimedia Project	PBS Web Site Web or Multimedia Authoring Software	✓				
Multimedia Portfolio	Web or Multimedia Authoring Software	✓	✓	✓	✓	✓
PowerPoint Presentation	Microsoft PowerPoint	✓	✓	✓	✓	✓
Primary Source Documents Research	Online Research Resources					✓
Programming	Text Editor and Online Resources for Research				✓	✓

Instructional Strategy	Technology	English Language Learners	Physical Disabilities	Cognitive Disabilities	Learning Disabilities	Gifted and Talented
Science Experiments With GPS	Global Positioning Receiver				✓	✓
Searching World Wide Web	Access to World Wide Web	✓	✓	✓	✓	✓
Storyboard	Paper and Pen	✓	✓	✓	✓	✓
Teaching the Pythagorean Theorem With Calculator	Calculator			✓	✓	
Time-Lapse Photography	Digital Camera			✓	✓	✓
Video-Based Book Report	Video Camera Video Editing System (iMac)	✓	✓	✓	✓	✓
Virtual Expeditions	Web Access	✓	✓	✓	✓	✓
Web-Based Portfolio	Web Authoring Software Digital Camera	✓	✓	✓	✓	✓
Word Webs	Kidspiration		✓	✓	✓	
Writing an E-Book	MeBooks	✓	✓	✓	✓	✓

References and Suggested Readings

CHAPTER 1

Butler-Pascoe, M. E., & Wiburg, K. (2003). *Technology and teaching English language learners.* Boston: Allyn & Bacon.

Giangreco, M. F., Cloninger, C. J., Dennis, R. E., & Edelman, S. W. (2000). Problem-solving methods to facilitate inclusive education. In R. A. Vila & J. S. Thousand (Eds.), *Restructuring for caring and effective education: Piecing the puzzle together* (2nd ed.). Baltimore: Brookes.

Gilley, J. (2002). Gender and technology awareness training in preservice teacher education. *TechTrends, 46*(6), 21–26.

Heward, W. L. (2003). *Exceptional children: An introduction to special education.* Columbus, OH: Pearson Education, Inc.

Honey, M., Moeller, B., Brunner, C., Bennett, D., Clements, P., & Hawkins, J. (1991, Fall). Girls and design: Exploring the question of technological imagination. *Transformations 2*(2).

International Center for Disability Resources on the Internet. (1999). Applying the ADA to the Internet: A web accessibility standard. Retrieved August 6, 2003, from http://www.icdri.org/constructing_accessible_web_site.htm.

International Society for Technology in Education. (2000). *National educational technology standards for students.* Eugene, OR: ISTE.

Margolis, J., & Fisher, A. (2001). *Unlocking the clubhouse: Women in computing.* Cambridge, MA: MIT Press.

Mathis, S. G. (2002). Improving first-year women undergraduates' perceptions of their computer skills. *TechTrends, 46*(6), 27–29.

National Center for Education Statistics. (2003). NCES fast facts. Retrieved April 24, 2003, from http://nces.ed.gov/fastfacts/display.asp?id=96.

Schrum, L., & Geisler, S. (2003). Gender issues and considerations. In G. Solomon, N. Allen, & P. Resta (Eds.), *Toward digital equity.* Arlington Heights, IL: Allyn and Bacon.

U.S. Department of Education. (2002). Twenty-third annual report to Congress on the implementation of the Individuals with Disabilities Education Act. Washington, DC: Author.

U.S. Department of Education. (2003). IDEA'97: What's new! Retrieved August 6, 2003, from http://www.ed.gov/offices/OSERS/Policy/IDEA/regs.html.

CHAPTER 2

Butler-Pascoe, M. E., & Wiburg, K. (2003). *Technology and teaching English language learners.* Boston: Allyn & Bacon.

Diaz, C. F. (2001). The third millennium: A multicultural imperative for education. In C. F. Diaz (Ed.), *Multicultural education in the 21st century* (pp. 1–10). New York: Longman.

ERIC Digests. (1993, November 1). Retrieved June 19, 2003, from http://www.ericfacility.net/ericdigests/ed377138.html.

Fombonne, E. (1999). The epidemiology of autism: A review. *Psychological Medicine, 29,* 769–786.

Friend, M., & Bursuck, W. (1996). *Including students with special needs: A practical guide for classroom teachers.* Boston: Allyn & Bacon.

Guilford, J. P. (1987). Creativity research: Past, present and future. In S. Isakesen (Ed.), *Frontiers of creativity research* (pp. 33–66). Buffalo, NY: Bearly.

Hallahan, D. P., & Kauffman, J. M. (2000). *Exceptional learners: Introduction to special education* (8th ed.). Boston: Allyn and Bacon.

Heward, W. L. (2003). *Exceptional children: An introduction to special education* (7th ed.). Boston: Pearson Education, Inc.

International Dyslexia Association. (2002, November 12). Retrieved June 20, 2003, from http://www.interdys.org/servlet/compose?section_id=5&page_id=95.

Lutkenhoff, M. (Ed.). (1999). *Children with spina bifida: A parents' guide.* Bethesda, MD: Woodbine.

Lutkenhoff, M., & Oppenheimer, S. (1997). *SPINAbilities: A young person's guide to spina bifida.* Bethesda, MD: Woodbine.

McLone, D. (1998). *An introduction to spina bifida.* Washington, DC: Spina Bifida Association of America.

National Center for Learning Disabilities. (2003). Retrieved June 20, 2003, from http://www.ld.org/info/indepth/dyscalculia.cfm.

National Information Center for Children and Youth with Disabilities. (2003). Retrieved February 5, 2004, from http://www.nichcy.org/.

National Joint Committee on Learning Disabilities. (1989, September 18). Letter from NJCLD to member organizations. Topic: Modification to the NJCLD definition of learning disabilities.

National Spinal Chord Injury Association. (2001). *Facts and figures.* Birmingham: University of Alabama.

Office of Special Education and Rehabilitative Services. (1997). Retrieved June 20, 2003, from http://www.ed.gov/offices/OSERS/Policy/IDEA/IDEA.pdf.

Sandler, A. (1997). *Living with spina bifida: A guide for families and professionals.* Chapel Hill, NC: University of North Carolina Press.

Shore, K. (1998). *Special kids problem solver: Ready-to-use interventions for helping all students with academic, behavioral, and physical problems.* Boston: Prentice-Hall.

References and Suggested Readings ● 91

Shaklee, B., Whitmore, J., Barton, L., Barbour, N., Ambross, R., & Viechnicki, K. (1989). *Early assessment for exceptional potential for young and/or economically disadvantaged students.* Washington, DC: Office of Educational Research and Improvement, U.S. Department of Education Grant No. R206A00160.

Thompson, M. S., Dicerbo, K. E., Mahoney, K., & MacSwan, J. (2002). Exito en California?: A validity critique of language program evaluations and analysis of English learner test scores. Retrieved from the World Wide Web March 29, 2004: http://epaa.asu.

U.S. Department of Education. (1998). *Twenty-first annual report to Congress on the implementation of the Individuals with Disabilities Education Act.* Washington, DC: Author.

U.S. Department of Education. (2002*). Twenty-fourth annual report to Congress on the implementation of the Individuals with Disabilities Education Act.* Washington, DC: Author.

Ybarra, R., & Green, T. (2003). Using technology to help ESL/EFL students develop language skills. *The Internet TESL Journal, 9*(3). Retrieved May 25, 2003, from http://iteslj.org/Articles/Ybarra-Technology.html.

CHAPTER 3

Accommodating persons with hearing impairments. Retrieved June 20, 2003, from http://cio.doe.gov/assistive/hearing.html.

Accommodating persons with physical impairments. Retrieved June 20, 2003, from http://cio.doe.gov/assistive/physical.html.

Accommodating persons with visual impairments. Retrieved June 20, 2003, from http://cio.doe.gov/assistive/visual.html.

AlphaSmart, Inc. (2003). AlphaSmart 3000. Retrieved June 20, 2003, from http://www.alphasmart.com/products/as3000_overview.html.

AltaVista. (2003). AltaVista's Babel Fish Translation Service. Retrieved June 22, 2003, from http://babelfish.altavista.com.

American Hearing Aid Associates. (2002). Hearing care tips for children: American Hearing Aid Associates. Retrieved June 20, 2003, from http://www.ahaanet.com/fmsystems.asp.

Assistive Technologies, Inc. (2002). Assistive Technologies, Inc.: About us. Retrieved June 20, 2003, from http://www.assistivetechnologies.com/about.htm.

Broderbund. (2001). Broderbund home page. Retrieved June 22, 2003, from http://www.broderbund.com/broderbund.asp.

Center for Effective Collaboration and Practice. (2003). Center for Effective Collaboration and Practice. Retrieved June 22, 2003, from http://cecp.air.org/.

Enabling Technologies. (2003). Braille printers from Enabling Technologies. Retrieved June 20, 2003, from http://www.brailler.com.

Freedom Scientific. (2003). Products and Services: Jaws for Windows. Retrieved June 20, 2003, from http://www.freedomscientific.com/fs_products/software_jaws.asp.

Greystone Digital, Inc. (2002). The BigKeys Company home page. Retrieved June 20, 2003, from http://www.bigkeys.com/html/bigkeys_1level.html.

Hallahan, D. P., & Kauffman, J. M. (2000). *Exceptional learners: Introduction to special education* (8th ed.). Boston: Allyn & Bacon.

IBM Corporation. (2003a). IBM Accessibility Center. Retrieved June 22, 2003, from http://www-3.ibm.com/able.

IBM Corporation. (2003b). IBM ViaVoice for Windows and Macintosh. Retrieved June 20, 2003, from http://www-3.ibm.com/software/speech/.

In Touch Systems. (2003). The Magic Wand Keyboard. Retrieved June 20, 2003, from http://www.magicwandkeyboard.com/.

IntelliTools. (2003a). The IntelliKeys programmable keyboard. Retrieved June 20 2003, from http://www.intellitools.com/Products/IntelliKeys/home.htm.

IntelliTools. (2003b). IntelliTools math products. Retrieved June 20 2003, from http://www.intellitools.com/Products/itmath_products.htm.

iVisit. (2003). iVisit LLC. Retrieved June 20, 2003, from http://www.ivisit.info/front/images4/front4.php.

Michigan State University Artificial Language Laboratory. (2002). SCATIR Switch page. Retrieved June 20, 2003, from http://www.msu.edu/~artlang/SCATIR.html#Introduction.

Microsoft. (2002). NetMeeting home page. Retrieved June 20, 2003, from http://www.microsoft.com/windows/netmeeting/default.asp.

Riverdeep Interactive Learning Limited. (2003). Riverdeep Interactive Learning. Retrieved June 22, 2003, from http://www.riverdeep.net.

SDL International. (2003). FreeTranslation.com—free translation from English to Spanish, French, German, Italian, Dutch. Retrieved June 22, 2003, from http://www.freetranslation.com/web.htm.

Southwest Educational Development Laboratory. (2003). *Assistive technologies for students with learning disabilities.* Retrieved June 20, 2003, from http://www.sedl.org/rural/seeds/assistivetech/atld.html.

Steele-Carlin, S. (2001). *Assistive devices help challenged kids get the most from learning.* Retrieved June 20, 2003, from http://www.educationworld.com/a_tech/tech086.shtml.

Text to Speech Software.Com. (2002). Text to Speech Software: Text reader. Retrieved June 20, 2003, from http://www.text-to-speech-software.com/.

Translation Experts Limited. (2003). InterTran. Retrieved June 22, 2003, from http://www.intertran.net/.

U.S. Department of Energy. (2003a). *Current and emerging assistive technologies: Physical assistive technologies.* Retrieved November 14, 2003, from http://cio.doe.gov/assistive/physical.html.

U.S. Department of Energy. (2003b). *Current and emerging assistive technologies: Hearing assistive technologies.* Retrieved November 14, 2003, from http://cio.doe.gov/assistive/hearing.html.

CHAPTER 4

Bolt, D. B., & Crawford, R. A. K. (2000). Digital divide: Computers and our children's future. New York: TVBooks.

Brown, K. (1993). Balancing the tools of technology with our own humanity: The use of technology in building partnerships and communities. In J. V. Tinagero & A. F. Ada (Eds.), *The power of two languages: Literacy and biliteracy for Spanish-speaking students* (pp. 178–198). New York: Macmillan/McGraw-Hill.

Butler-Pascoe, M. E., & Wiburg, K. M. (2003). *Technology and teaching English language learners.* Boston: Allyn & Bacon.

Gilley, J. (2002). Gender and technology awareness training in preservice teacher education. *TechTrends, 46*(6), 21–26.

Green, T. (2001). Virtual expeditions: Taking your students around the world without leaving the classroom. *The Social Studies, 92*(4), 177–179.

Green, T., & Peerless, J. (2001). Digital MeBooks: Using HyperStudio with English as second language students. *Leading and Learning with Technology, 29*(2), 32–35, 56.

Hoffman, D. L., & Novak, T. P. (1998, April 17). Bridging the racial divide on the Internet. *Science.*

Liaw, M. L. (1997). An analysis of ESL children's verbal interaction during computer book reading. *Computers in the Schools, 13*(3/4), 55–73.

Margolis, J., & Fisher, A. (2001). *Unlocking the clubhouse: Women in computing.* Cambridge, MA: MIT Press.

Mathis, S. G. (2002). Improving first-year women undergraduates' perceptions of their computer skills. *TechTrends, 46*(6), 27–29.

National Center for Education Statistics. (2000, February). *Internet access in U.S. public schools and classrooms: 1994–99.* Washington, DC: US NCES. Retrieved August 10, 2003, from http://nces.ed.gov/pubs2000/2000086.pdf.

Neuman, D. (1994). Technology and equity. *NABE News, 18*(1), 17–18, 32.

Ovando, C. J., & Collier, V. P. (1998). *Bilingual and ESL classrooms* (2nd ed.). Boston: McGraw-Hill.

Pearson, T. (2001). Falling behind: A technology crisis facing minority students. *TechTrends, 46*(2), 15–20.

Tomlinson, C. A. (2001). *How to differentiate instruction in mixed-ability classrooms* (2nd ed.). Alexandria, VA: Association for Supervision and Curriculum Development.

Ybarra, R., & Green, T. (2003). Using technology to help ESL/EFL students develop language skills. *The Internet TESL Journal, 6*(3). Retrieved July 13, 2003, from http://iteslj.org/Articles/Ybarra-Technology.html.

Index

ADA. *See* Americans with Disabilities Act
AlphaSmart, 43
Ambross, R., 30, 90
Americans with Disabilities Act
    description of, 7, 12, 16
    web site accessibility guidelines, 16
Antisocial behavior, 26
Aphasia, 9
Art instruction, 65–67
Ask an expert, 72–73
Assistive/adaptive technologies
    augmentative and alternative
        communication devices, 42–43
    characteristics of, 34
    computers
        eye movement activation switch, 38
        input devices, 35–39
        keyboards, 35–37
        mouse, 35, 38
        output devices, 39–40
        speech recognition, 37
        speech synthesizers, 40, 44
        tactile output, 39
        word prediction packages, 37
    definition of, 10
    hardware-related, 34–43
    hearing aids, 42
    Internet-based communication, 40–41
    software-related, 43–46
    summary overview of, 51
    telephone systems, 41–42
    types of, 34
    web site resources for, 52
Attention deficit hyperactivity
    disorder, 9
Audio recordings, 68
Augmentative and alternative
    communication devices, 42–43
Autism, 24–25

Barbour, N., 30, 90
Barton, L., 30, 90
Behavior(s)
    antisocial, 26
    cultural influences on, 5
    "female," 5
    "male," 5
    in mentally retarded students, 25
Behavioral disorders
    description of, 26
    remediation software for students
        with, 48
Bennett, D., 5, 89
Blindness, 23
Bolt, D. B., 59, 92
Boys
    computing technology use by, 5–6, 63
    socially constructed behaviors, 5
Braille markers, 37
Brown, K., 62, 92
Brunner, C., 5, 89
Bursuck, W., 22, 25, 28, 90
Butler-Pascoe, M. E., 5, 20, 62, 89–90, 92

Calculators, 49, 70
Captioning, 39, 45
Center for Applied Special
    Technology, 52
Center for Assistive Technology, 52
Cerebral palsy, 21–22
Classroom
    inclusive, 55–56
    success in, 2
    technology integration in, 2
Clements, P., 5, 89
Cloninger, C. J., 15, 89
Closed captioning, 45
Closed-circuit television camera, 39
Cognitive impairment, 8–9, 24

Collier, V. P., 61, 93
Communication
  disorders of, 27
  Internet use for, 40–41, 63
  nonverbal, 67
Compensatory technologies
  calculators, 49
  description of, 10, 48–49, 52
Comprehension instruction, 65
Computers
  access to, 2
  assistive/adaptive technologies
    input devices, 35–38
    keyboards, 35–37
    monitors, 39
    output devices, 39–40
    speech synthesizers, 40, 44
    tactile output, 39
    touch screens, 36
  English Language Learners
    use of, 61
  filmmaking uses of, 6
  gifted and talented student's use of,
    50–51
Council for Exceptional Children, 17
Crawford, R. A. K., 59, 92
Creativity, 30
Cultural differences. See also English
    Language Learners
  assessment of, 4
  description of, 3
  measures of, 3–4
Cultural sensitivity, 59–60

Data gathering and manipulation, 72
Deafness, 24
Dennis, R. E., 15, 89
Diaz, C. F., 20, 90
Dicerbo, 21
Differences
  challenges associated with, 2
  cultural. See Cultural differences
  recognition of, 2
Differentiated instruction
  description of, 54–55
  example of, 57–59
  for minorities, 60
Digital books, 69
Digital divide
  definition of, 59
  description of, 2–3
  minorities affected by, 59–60
Digital manipulatives, 70

Disability
  definition of, 7–8
  groups of, 8
  inclusion approach, 14–15
  learning. See Learning disabilities
  legislation regarding, 11–12
Diverse learners
  cognitively impaired students,
    8–9, 24
  English Language Learners, 20–21
  gifted and talented students. See Gifted
    and talented students
  impairments. See Impairment(s)
  Internet resources for, 31–32
  learning disabilities. See Learning
    disabilities
  physically impaired students. See
    Physical impairments
  professional development opportunities
    for dealing with, 32
Dyscalculia, 29–30
Dysgraphia, 29, 49
Dyslexia, 8, 28–29

Edelman, S. W., 15, 89
Education for All Handicapped
    Children, 11
ELL. See English Language Learners
E-mail, 40
Emotions, 66
English Language Learners
  characteristics of, 60–61
  classroom integration difficulties for, 61
  computer use by, 61
  difficulties experienced by, 20, 61
  group work by, 62
  instructional environment for, 61
  needs of, 20–21
  percentage of, 20
  state-imposed limitations on, 20–21
  strategies for, 21
  technology use by, 21, 60–63
  translation software for, 45–46
English language proficiency
    assessments, 4
Enhancement software, 46
Exceptional children
  differences among, 7
  in inclusive classroom, 56
  legislation to protect, 11–12
  percentage of, 10–11, 21
  terms for describing, 8
  types of, 8–9

Exceptional Learners Education Web, 31
Expressive math, 71
Extension technologies, 50–51
Eye movement activation switch, 38

Feelings, 66
Fine motor skill development, 66
Fisher, A., 6, 63, 89, 93
Fombonne, E., 25, 90
Formative assessments, 55
Freeware, 43
Friend, M., 22, 25, 28, 90
Functionally blind, 23

Geisler, S., 5, 89
Gender
    influences on, 5–6
    teacher's awareness of, 6
    technology use based on, 63–64
Giangreco, M. F., 15, 89
Gifted and Talented Children's Education
        Act of 1978, 12
Gifted and talented students
    characteristics of, 30
    computer use by, 50–51
    creativity of, 30
    definition of, 9
    definitions of, 30
    extension technologies for, 50–51
    with learning disabilities, 27
    state-sponsored services for, 11
Gilley, J., 2, 6, 63, 89, 92
Girls
    classroom management strategies
        for, 64
    computing technology use by, 5–6, 63–64
    encouragement of, 63–64
    socially constructed behaviors, 5
Glare protection screens, 39
Graphic arts, 6
Green, T., 21, 61, 91–93
Guilford, J. P., 30, 90

Hallahan, D. P., 21, 24, 26, 28, 42, 90
Handicapped, 7
Hands-free control devices, 38
Hawkins, J., 5, 89
Hearing aids, 42
Hearing impairment, 23–24
Heward, W. L., 11, 21–26, 28, 30, 89
Higher-order thinking skills, 66
Hoffman, D. L., 59, 92
Honey, M., 5, 89

IDEA. See Individuals with Disabilities
        Education Act
IEP. See Individual education plan
Impairment(s)
    autism, 24–25
    behavioral disorders, 26
    cognitive, 8–9, 24
    communication disorders, 27
    computer keyboard adaptations for,
        35–37
    computer mouse adaptations
        for, 35, 38
    definition of, 7–8
    mental retardation, 25–26
    physical. See Physical impairments
    software technologies for, 44
    speech, 27
    visual, 23
    web site accessibility, 16
Inclusion
    definition of, 14
    description of, 12
    in educational settings, 15
Inclusive classroom, 55–56
Individual education plan
    components of, 13, 56
    creation of, 13, 56
    description of, 12, 16
    least restrictive environment principle
        of, 12, 14
    modifications specified in, 13–14
    progress assessments in, 14
    teacher's role in, 13, 56
    technology included in, 57–58
Individualized instruction, 55
Individuals with Disabilities
        Education Act
    learning disability as defined by, 28
    mental retardation as defined by, 25
    principles of, 11–12, 16
    technology guidelines in, 15–16
    web site for, 32
Information technology, 6
Input/output devices, 35
Instant Messenger, 40
Instruction
    art, 65–67
    differentiated, 54–55
    individualized, 55
    language arts, 67–69
    mathematics, 69–71
    qualitative, 55
    science, 71–73

social studies, 73–76
strategies, 86–88
IntelliKeys, 35–36
International Society for Technology in
    Education, 15
Internet. *See also* Web sites
    classroom uses of, 73
    communication uses of, 40–41, 63
    interactions with other students using, 63
    resources available using, 12
    translation software for web sites, 46
ISTE. *See* International Society for
    Technology in Education

Kauffman, J. M., 21, 24, 26, 28, 42, 90
Keyboard adaptations, 35–37
Keyguard, 38
Key-pals, 74
Key repeat rate control, 36

Language arts instruction, 67–69
Learning Bridges Online Learning
    Center, 17
Learning disabilities
    computer technology for
        keyboard adaptations, 35–37
        mouse adaptations, 35, 38
        software, 49
    criteria for, 28
    definitions of, 27–28
    description of, 27
    dyscalculia, 29–30
    dysgraphia, 29, 49
    dyslexia, 28–29
    in gifted and talented students, 27
    Individuals with Disabilities Education
        Act definition of, 28
    National Joint Committee on Learning
        Disabilities definition of, 28
    percentage of, 11
    prevalence of, 27
    types of, 28–30
Learning supportive technologies
    characteristics of, 34
    compensatory, 48–50
    description of, 46–47
    extension, 50–51
    remediation, 47–48
Least restrictive environment, 12, 55–56
Legislation, for disabilities, 11–12
Lesson plans, 77
Liaw, M. L., 61, 93
Life skills software, 47

Limited English Proficiency, 4
Logical thinking, 70–71
LRE. *See* Least restrictive environment
Lutkenhoff, M., 22, 90

Macros, 36
Manipulatives, 70
Margolis, J., 6, 63, 89, 93
Mathematics instruction, 69–71
Mathis, S. G., 63, 89, 93
McLone, D., 22, 90
Mental retardation, 25–26
Minorities. *See also* English Language
        Learners
    differentiated instruction for, 60
    digital divide effects on, 59–60
    technology access for, 59–60
Moeller, B., 5, 89
MOOs, 51
Motor skill development, 66
Mouse, 35, 38
MUDs, 51
Muscular dystrophy, 22

*National Educational Technology Standards
    for Students*, 15
National Joint Committee on Learning
    Disabilities, 28
Neuman, D., 61, 93
NJCLD. *See* National Joint
        Committee on Learning
        Disabilities
Nonverbal communication, 67
Novak, T. P., 59, 92

Oppenheimer, S., 22, 90
Optical character recognition
    software, 45
Organizational software, 49
Ovando, C. J., 61, 93

Pearson, T., 59, 93
Peerless, J., 92
Physical impairments
    cerebral palsy, 21–22
    definition of, 8–9
    hearing impairment, 23–24
    muscular dystrophy, 22
    software technologies for, 44
    spina bifida, 22
    spinal cord injuries, 22–23
    traumatic brain injury, 24
    visual impairment, 23

Prewriting, 67
Primary source documents, 75–76
Programming languages, 70–71

Qualitative instruction, 55

Rehabilitation Engineering and
    Assistive Technology Society of
    North America, 52
Remedial technologies, 10
Remediation, software programs
    for, 47–48
Robotic devices, 37–38, 72

Sandler, A., 22, 90
Schrum, L., 5, 89
Science instruction, 71–73
Sequential keystroke input, 36
Shaklee, B., 30, 90
Shareware, 43
Shore, K., 20–21, 90
Social studies instruction, 73–76
Socioeconomic status
    experiences affected by, 4
    technology use based on, 4–5
Software
    assistive/adaptive, 43–46
    classification of, 43
    "drill and practice," 61
    enhancement, 46
    freeware, 43
    life skills, 47
    optical character recognition, 45
    organizational, 49
    remediation programs, 47–48
    shareware, 43
    speech-to-text, 45
    text-to-speech, 44
    translation, 43–46, 61
Speech impairments, 27
Speech recognition, 37
Speech synthesizers, 40, 44
Speech-to-text software, 45
Spina bifida, 22
Spinal cord injuries, 22–23
Spreadsheets, 71
Standards, 15–16
States
    English Language Learners limitations
        imposed by, 20–21
    gifted and talented student services
        offered by, 11
Steele-Carlin, S., 34, 92

Students
    frustration for, 2
    physically impaired. See Physical
        impairments

Teachers
    gender issues and, 6
    individual education plan development
        by, 13, 56
    least restrictive environment
        effects on, 12
    online resources for, 31–32
    professional development opportunities
        for, 32
Teaching Diverse Learners, 17
Technology
    access to, 2, 60
    art instruction using, 65–67
    assistive/adaptive. See
        Assistive/adaptive technologies
    classroom integration of, 2
    compensatory, 48–50, 52
    definition of, 33
    developmentally appropriate material
        made more appealing using, 50
    for English Language Learners, 21
    extension, 50–51
    gender differences, 5, 63–64
    guidelines for, 15–16
    individual education plan provision for,
        57–58
    "innovative," 33
    language arts instruction using, 67–69
    learning supportive. See Learning
        supportive technologies
    mathematics instruction using, 69–71
    minorities' access to, 59–60
    remediation, 47–48
    science instruction using, 71–73
    social studies instruction using, 73–76
    standards for, 15–16
    types of, 79–83
Telephone systems, 41–42
Teletypewriter devices, 41
Text-to-speech software, 44
Time-lapse photography, 73
Tomlinson, C. A., 93
Touch screens, 36
Translation software, 43–46, 61
Traumatic brain injury, 24

Veichnicki, 30, 90
Video recordings, 68

Virtual expeditions, 74–75
Visual impairments
    description of, 23
    software technologies for, 46

Web sites. *See also* Internet
    accessibility to, 16
    assistive/adaptive technologies, 52
    lesson plans, 77
    professional resources, 76–77
    translation software for, 46, 61

Whitmore, J., 30, 90
Wiburg, K., 5, 20, 62, 89–90, 92
Word prediction packages, 37
Word processing
    benefits of, 9–10
    language arts instruction
        using, 68
    writing tool use of, 48–49
Word recognition reading practice, 69

Ybarra, R., 21, 61, 91, 93

CORWIN PRESS

The Corwin Press logo—a raven striding across an open book—represents the union of courage and learning. Corwin Press is committed to improving education for all learners by publishing books and other professional development resources for those serving the field of K–12 education. By providing practical, hands-on materials, Corwin Press continues to carry out the promise of its motto: **"Helping Educators Do Their Work Better."**

Mack Wilberg is the Music Director of the Mormon Tabernacle Choir. He was appointed Music Director in March of 2008, having served as Associate Music Director since May 1999. He is a former professor of music at Brigham Young University, where he received his bachelor's degree; his master's and doctoral degrees are from the University of Southern California.

Alongside his conducting responsibilities he is active as a pianist, choral clinician, composer, arranger, and guest conductor throughout the United States and abroad. In addition to the many compositions he has written for the Mormon Tabernacle Choir, his works have been performed by artists such as Renée Fleming, Frederica von Stade, Bryn Terfel, The King's Singers, and narrators Walter Cronkite, Claire Bloom, Michael York, and Jane Seymour. Wilberg's arrangements and compositions are performed and recorded all over the world.

Have you tried?

America the Beautiful ·	(ISBN 978-0-19-386812-0)
Deep River	(ISBN 978-0-19-386919-6)
I'm runnin' on	(ISBN 978-0-19-386987-5)
Peace Like a River	(ISBN 978-0-19-386814-4)
Shenandoah (SATB)	(ISBN 978-0-19-386820-5)

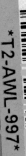

OXFORD
UNIVERSITY PRESS

www.oup.com

ISBN 978-0-19-339476-6

9 780193 394766

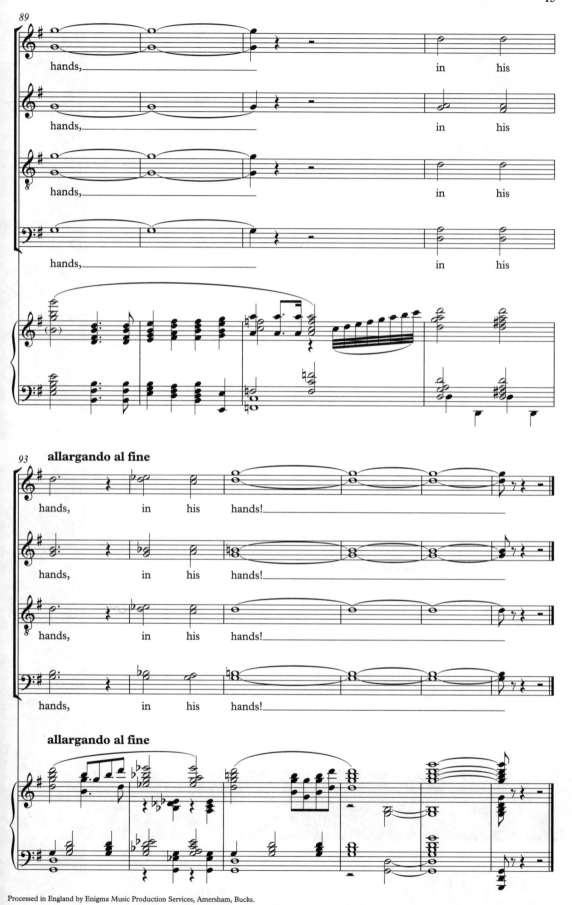

FORD

SATB choir and piano

Mack Wilberg

He's got the whole world in his hands

oxford spirituals

for the Mormon Tabernacle Choir and Orchestra at Temple Square

He's got the whole world in his hands

African-American Spiritual
arr. **MACK WILBERG**

The melody should always be phrased as marked in the first verse, with a breath after 'hands'.

An accompaniment for orchestra (3fl (+picc), 2ob, 2cl, 2bsn, 4hn, 3tpt, 3tbn, tba, timp, 3perc (tri, susp cym, BD, chimes), hp, org, r) is available on hire/rental from the publisher or appropriate agent.

Also available in an arrangement for men's voices (TTBB) (ISBN 978-0-19-339477-3). The TTBB version has been recorded by e Mormon Tabernacle Choir and Orchestra at Temple Square on the CD *Men of the Mormon Tabernacle Choir* (SKU 5053126).

Oxford University Press 2013

Printed in the USA

OXFORD UNIVERSITY PRESS, MUSIC DEPARTMENT, GREAT CLARENDON STREET, OXFORD OX2 6DP

4

in his   hands, he's got the whole   world   in his   hands, he's got the

whole world in his   hands.